Ready To Talk

Ready To Talk

A Companion Guide To Psychotherapy

Mary Sanger, LMFT, LPC, LCDC

Insights Publishing Company
Dallas, Texas

ISBN: 069246591X
ISBN 9780692465912

Insights Publishing Company
Dallas, Texas

ACKNOWLEDGEMENTS

My journey into the field of psychology didn't begin until later in my life and would not have happened at all if it had not been for the encouragement and support of certain people. To them I am forever grateful. One such person is Dr. Marc Rathbun who encouraged and inspired me to believe in my abilities to be a therapist long before I did.

When I began my graduate work, I was lucky enough in my first semester to have as my professor Dr. Michael Leach. Had it not been so, I'm not sure I would have stuck it out. He helped me to commit my vision to paper, which I still think about almost daily, and he spent many hours just talking, listening, and thinking together with me.

To the great many brilliant men and women in the field of psychology that came before me, I honor and thank you for your research, study, and healing skills. The ideas put forth in this book are really an eclectic gathering of your theories and practices that have proven to be helpful to so many in my practice.

The spark to write this book came from my colleagues at Insights Collaborative Therapy Group. Thank you for believing that I had something worth sharing and committing to paper. I enjoy going to the office each and every day in large part because of you - the collaboration, the inspiration, and the friendship you give.

To my good friend Kristin Cicciarelli, whose commitment to seeing this project through to the end is appreciated more than she will ever know. We are sisters for life.

To Laurence Sanger, my husband, my friend, my partner, and the yang to my yin. What an unbelievably great life we have together. We have shared love and laughter that was totally unknown to me before you. Your support and belief in me has allowed me to grow and discover new heights. You are totally frogly, but a perfect frog for me. Know that you are profoundly admired and deeply loved.

Lastly to my clients, fellow travelers in life, for whom and because of whom this book is written. I thank you for allowing me to accompany you on your journey.

AUTHOR'S NOTE

For the purpose of easier reading, I have opted to use "he" and "him" when referring to the client, rather than what I believe is the more cumbersome "she/he", "her/him" or "they/them."

CONTENTS

I prefer to think of my patients and myself as fellow travelers, a term that abolishes distinctions between 'them' (the afflicted) and 'us' (the healers)... We are all in this together and there is no therapist and no person immune to the inherent tragedies of existence.

-Irvin Yalom, *The Gift Of Therapy*

INTRODUCTION

Remember the movie *Groundhog Day*? In this popular 90's comedy, the main character, an arrogant local TV weatherman played by Bill Murray, finds himself in a comedic time loop, doomed to repeat the exact same day over and over. In a vain attempt to break the endless repetitive cycle, Murray's character, Phil Connors, behaves outrageously, knowing that his actions have no long-term consequences. No matter what he does, tomorrow morning he will be right back where he is today: February 2. As the movie progresses, Phil gradually evolves from a miserable jerk into a happy, fulfilled man involved in a meaningful romantic relationship with Rita, played by Andie MacDowell. Murray's gradual transformation comes when he realizes through conversations with Rita that he is not a victim of life's circumstances but the author of the story of his own life. *Groundhog Day* is a poignant reminder that each of us, and without the constraints of a time loop, has the same opportunity for growth and happiness as does Murray's character. Perhaps you're putting up with an unsatisfying job, unfulfilling relationships, or living less than the life you want – all because you don't know how to change or, in some cases, because you don't even know you *can* change.

But somewhere deep down inside, you want that change. You sense that your life can and should be better than it currently is. The fact that you're reading this book demonstrates desire and willingness to change.

As a psychotherapist, I commend you for your decision to use therapy as a tool for helping you make change in your life. I want you to know that although the therapeutic journey can be a highly challenging one, it's one that promises reward beyond measure. Though you may be feeling scared or at least uncertain what to expect during therapy, you've come to the realization that life is a precious gift and far too short to be spent complaining and reliving the same pain or joylessness day in and day out. You've come to the right place to find out what therapy can potentially do for you, and what *you* can do to enhance its effectiveness.

It's true that you're the author of your own life story. What you may not realize is that both your resolved and unresolved past experiences unconsciously shape your current life stories and so unconsciously affect your decisions and the quality of your life. One important feature of therapy is that it can help make you consciously aware of some of those "hidden" experiences and transform them from emotionally powerful negative influences into wispy memories. Therapy can help free you from the past so that you can more fully experience and enjoy the present and sow the seeds of a better future.

Each of us has a story to tell based on our family of origin (which means the *family* that you grew up in — your parents, siblings and perhaps grandparents or other relatives who lived with you during part of your childhood), experiences and relationships — both good and bad. It's a story we tell others certainly, but more importantly it's a story we tell ourselves. It's difficult to determine exactly how one person can use his story, even a painful one, to his advantage while another allows it to define and prevent him from moving forward. But it's the latter who typically ends up in my office — someone who knows he isn't living on preferred terms, who wants to *enjoy* life rather than trudge through it, and has perhaps tried to improve his situation previously without much success. He may come alone or with a spouse, partner or family member(s) with whom he is struggling to relate. He may feel stuck, frustrated and even miserable, and just can't see how he can possibly change course.

Regardless of your past, you've come to the point where you're no longer willing to carry its burden with you. Though you may not know yet how to extract yourself from your story and to write new chapters, you realize that your old story is no longer serving you. "That's just who I am" is ready to make way for "This is who I want to be." The time has come for you to debunk the myths that your past will always hold you back because deep in your heart you know if you don't, you're doomed to repeat it.

The name of this book, *Ready to Talk*, indicates desired movement toward change: the type of change that opens new chapters, closes old ones and offers a greater understanding of self. Your decision to employ psychotherapy as a tool for both *feeling* and *getting* better is the first step in ridding yourself of debilitating emotional pain — pain that was deep enough for you to schedule an appointment with a therapist.

There are many different paths to emotional health — talk therapy is one of those ways. There are also many different approaches to therapy. In this book I will share the type of therapy that I practice and that my clients find instrumental in their healing process.

Talk therapy can be used among other things to reveal destructive behavioral patterns, create healthy boundaries (or redesign those that are no longer working) and aid you in discovering your authentic self. It's an investment in your mental and emotional health that has the ability to yield very high returns. But therapy is not a quick fix; it's a learning process. It's not designed to magically and instantaneously make all of your problems disappear; rather, it gradually teaches you new ways of thinking. Instead of trying to control and change the people and situations around you (which, by now, hopefully you're beginning to realize is a fruitless endeavor), therapy teaches you to see problems as challenges, to consider others' perspectives as well as your own, and to view life in a more gentle, less judgmental way. Therapy also teaches you that feelings are neither "right" nor "wrong" — they're just feelings. However, for talk therapy to be its most effective, it requires a sincere commitment from you, and you must be willing to do the work that it takes to achieve optimal results.

Like a physical fitness trainer, a therapist works with you, side by side, while you "exercise" — only in this case it's not physical exercise you're performing but mental and emotional. If you hired a fitness trainer at a gym one hour a week, then went home and ate fried foods and ice cream every day and didn't work out again until the next session, you'd be highly disappointed in the results. Your home routine is just as important, if not more so, than the one hour at the gym; one good session each week will not make up for six days of poor dietary habits and couch potato behavior. This book will provide you with helpful homework assignments, exercises and thought-provoking questions that you will use to "work out" between therapy sessions.

In the telling of your personal story to a therapist, you often discover unrecognized fallacies, distorted thinking and destructive behavioral patterns that you've developed along the way. Clients may be surprised to learn that therapy sometimes provides more questions than answers. I tell clients that emotional well-being is more a circuitous route than a linear one — often compared to peeling back the layers of an onion, one layer at a time. It's something that requires more of the right (or creative) side of your brain, often weaving in and out, sometimes coming back to the issue(s) that you started out with — at times this happens during one session or perhaps it happens over the course of our relationship. Like peeling an onion, therapy may bring some tears along the way, but it's this gradual peeling that reveals and brings greater clarity to your authentic self. Be prepared to have your current self-beliefs challenged, and also ready to accept — or at least try out — new and sometimes unfamiliar thoughts and behavior. Some clients (especially those who are left-brain dominant) would probably feel more comfortable if I gave them an outline, or a To Do list, or even a magic pill that would solve their problems. However, it's in the very telling of your story to a therapist that allows *you* the opportunity to rewrite it — one with greater clarity and acceptance of your true self.

This book was written with the first-time therapy client (or clients) in mind, whether in individual, relationship or family counseling, but it's not limited to that person. It's also designed for use by those who have experienced therapy and are ready to peel back another layer of the onion. This book will:

1. Explain how the therapeutic process works.
2. Enhance the therapeutic process for those undergoing regular psychotherapy. Remember the earlier comparison of the therapist to a personal trainer? Think of this book as a set of "squats", "lunges" and "sit-ups" that will help you achieve greater results in less time. Successful therapy is not just about the time you spend in your

therapist's office; the time you put into it outside the office is equally if not more important.

3. Help you cultivate a greater sense of your basic (authentic) self.

By the way, it's not uncommon for new clients to be unclear about their own likes and dislikes and their own wants and needs because they've covered up their true feelings for a lifetime or borrowed a sense of self from others rather than develop their own. In therapy, you will discover many of your true likes and dislikes, how to establish healthy boundaries and how to incorporate these things into your daily life.

I am excited for you that you're beginning this journey, and I am honored that you've invited me to join you. Let's start talking.

CHAPTER 1

"WHAT BRINGS YOU HERE?"

Why People Seek Therapy

The truth is that our finest moments are most likely to occur when we are feeling deeply uncomfortable, unhappy, or unfulfilled. For it is only in such moments, propelled by our discomfort, that we are likely to step out of our ruts and start searching for different ways or truer answers.
— M. Scott Peck

The title of this chapter wins the prize for "Most Frequently Asked Question" in any first therapy session (second prize probably goes to "And How Do You Feel About That?" but that one typically comes a bit later). It's the opening line of dialogue in what can be an enriching and ongoing conversation between client and therapist. It's also an invitation, encouraging you to begin sharing the burden of the problem or condition that is causing you enough unhappiness or pain to schedule an appointment.

The circumstances that prompt clients to seek therapy in the first place (called the "presenting problem") are usually some sort of emotional, mental, physical, spiritual, relational, sexual or financial problem. We may focus on that problem initially in therapy and that may be the essence of our work together. But in many cases, the presenting problem is just a doorway to deeper, more fundamental issues that become the subject of our therapy work.

In my profession, I encounter people every single day who come to me because they want to feel better. They may not understand why they feel so upset, unhappy or even miserable but they do know they just want to feel better. Perhaps they have become disillusioned by the notion that "something" (a new diet, a cosmetic procedure, a more expensive car or home, a new business or financial endeavor, a new relationship, alcohol, prescribed pharmaceutical drugs or other substances) was supposed to make them feel better but it just isn't working. By the time they reach my office, clients are beginning to realize that new possessions, new relationships or other quick fixes haven't worked. They want real and lasting results. But these results take time — time to learn new ways of thinking, new behavior patterns and to develop a greater sense of self. As a therapist, this is an exciting thing to witness and without a doubt, one of the most rewarding components of my job.

Why People Seek Talk Therapy

Therapy focuses on many things, but some of the more familiar subjects are:

- Behaviors
- Emotions
- Thoughts
- Conscious and unconscious motivations
- Family dynamics
- Relationship interactions
- Healing from past trauma

Initially, clients might not be able to identify exactly what is troubling them. But when I ask what brings them to my office, their answers typically fall into one of three categories:

1. "I feel (fill in the blank)." You're struggling with one or more mood-related disorders such as depression, stress, anxiety, obsessive/compulsive disorder, panic attacks, phobias and the like.
2. Relationship concerns. These may be with a current or ex-spouse or partner, family, parents, co-parent or co-worker. You may tell me that

you can't get along with some of these people or that you keep making the same mistakes in relationships and need to figure out why. It's not unusual for external factors such as a "manipulative mother", "cheating husband", "bad financial luck" or "aging parent" to be a part of your concerns.

3. Acting out. This may include drug, food, alcohol or behavioral addiction (like gambling, spending or work), sexual infidelity, explosive anger or recklessness. You may be in my office of your own accord or at someone else's suggestion or insistence. In this scenario, it's not uncommon for a precipitating (and perhaps unfortunate) event to have occurred such as the loss or potential loss of a relationship, job, child custody, etc. — something important enough to provoke you to take action.

Let's look more closely at the three categories listed above.

"I Feel (Fill in the Blank)" – Mood-Related Disorders

Janine is an attractive twenty-five year old who works as an executive assistant in a large law firm. It's not her desired occupation but she has been unable to get into law school due to her less than stellar college record and entrance exam scores. Her parents, both attorneys, are very worried about her. She feels depressed and lonely, especially after the recent break-up of her two-year relationship with Dan, an investment banker. On weeknights following work, she often collapses on the couch where she sleeps fitfully until about 3 a.m., then moves to her bed where she still can't get much restful sleep.

Janine's friends have attempted to engage her in various social activities but she says her heart simply isn't in it. Her relationship with Dan was everything to her. When I ask her whether she believes her sadness is related primarily to her failed relationship, she emphatically replies *yes*; if only the relationship had lasted, she claims, everything would be pretty terrific.

As Janine and I develop our client-therapist relationship over the next several weeks, I learn more about her family — specifically, how successful they all are in Janine's eyes. Her parents are partners in their own thriving law firm. Her three siblings are well educated, financially secure and happily married with beautiful children. Janine feels shame about her current job and repeatedly assures me it's only temporary. Her family hasn't said anything about it but she knows she has disappointed them by not getting into law school.

During each of our sessions, I encourage Janine to do something before our next session that will give her pure, unadulterated joy — and it was not to have anything to do with her quest to get into graduate school, nor related to wistful memories of Dan. So she did. Some weeks she would rent a funny movie and eat ice cream; others, she would download a new song or take a long, relaxing bath. But more often than not, her joyful activity centered on art. She started a drawing journal, tried practicing meditative art and soon signed up for an art history class at a local community college.

Though Janine is surrounded by professional, business-oriented people, it became clear that's not who she is or where her interests lie. I noticed that even in the way she dressed — she always included something very unusual and creative. Janine wore very conservative, preppy-styled clothes such as khaki skirts and jackets but always paired them with brightly colored sandals, long, dangling jewelry or something arty that she had made herself. Clearly, there was an artist trying to get out.

It was obvious to me that Janine was not living her life authentically, instead borrowing her family's hopes and dreams and taking them on as her own. Many of us do the same thing. We reach adulthood believing certain things about ourselves because we have avoided doing the difficult work — figuring out or developing our own authentic self. It was no wonder that Janine felt tired and depressed all the time. Imagine how exhausting and frustrating it would be, expending all of your energy being what someone else wants you to be!

When you lack a developed sense of self and instead take on others' ideas of whom we *ought* to be, you turn to outside things (others' opinions, material possessions, job titles, etc.) to define or validate you. As a result, you become highly concerned and focused on what others are doing or saying and depend on their approval. Often you begin to feel the need to control all of these outside influences so that they're favorable toward you. Exhausting, yes — but that is what many people do rather than focusing inward.

Workout

Are you living an authentic life? Ask yourself the following questions and see if any or all of them resonate with you:

- Do you often experience angry outbursts or crying jags for no apparent reason?
- Are you tired most of the time, even after a good night's sleep?
- Do you frequently engage in fantasies about how perfect life would be if you lost weight/found the right person/moved again/made more money/had a better job?
- Do you turn to food/alcohol/spending/drugs when you're depressed or upset?
- Do you change jobs/relationships/homes frequently?

When Janine first came to me, she was experiencing many of these symptoms. It was clear that she was allowing external factors and other people to determine her own life choices and happiness; when we do that, we will never find the answers we so desperately seek.

Relationship Concerns

Relationships, when healthy, provide us with love, nurturing and emotional support. They offer laughter or pleasure during happy times and bolster our strength during difficult ones. But when the relationship does not consist of two emotionally healthy, whole people, problems often arise.

Kerrie is a successful entrepreneur with adult children and a supportive husband, Trevor. They live a comfortable life — they've worked hard and are finally at a point where they can enjoy both their financial and personal freedom. There are no kids at home to worry about and their schedules are their own. Or at least they were until Trevor's mother, Sarah, moved in with them six months ago. Though Sarah is in reasonably good health for her age, Trevor believes that she is too fragile to live on her own. He is an only child and feels guilty that his mother has been alone since his father passed away.

Sarah is what some might call "a piece of work." She's highly critical of Kerrie's behavior, even when Kerrie is trying to be helpful towards Sarah. When Kerrie gets frustrated by her mother-in-law's antics, she tries to bite her tongue but isn't always successful. In her words, "You can bite your tongue for only so long before it starts bleeding!"

Kerrie and Trevor have been married for twenty-five years and while their marriage has been for the most part calm and communicative, they're now arguing several times a week — mostly about Sarah. They've come to me for couple's therapy because they're unable to develop a mutually agreed-upon solution for dealing with Sarah. During our first session together, indeed it's Sarah whose name comes up most frequently.

One of the things that I noticed during the first few sessions with Kerrie and Trevor is their communication style. Kerrie does most of the talking while Trevor looks like he'd rather be anywhere else on the planet. The only time he perks up is when Kerrie mentions a specific concern about his mother, to which Trevor typically responds, "That's not true" or "She's not always like that." I realize that one of the things we're going to need to explore is whether Trevor is emotionally fused to his mother in a way that is not helpful to his marriage. But first, we need to discover whether the lack of communication is a recent feature of their relationship (i.e., since Sarah moved in with them), or whether it has always been the case and perhaps they've not previously dealt with it.

I can see that Kerrie and Trevor care about each other. Trevor typically holds the door open for Kerrie and asks her if she would like tea from our office kitchen. Kerrie sometimes reaches over to take Trevor's hand. But I also notice that when Trevor disagrees with Kerrie's statements, she quickly shuts down. It's almost as if, if Trevor doesn't agree with what she says, then he automatically wins the debate — no discussion required.

When I ask the couple how they developed their plan for Sarah's stay with them, they look surprised. There really wasn't a plan, they tell me. Sarah suffered a minor fall and came to stay with them while she convalesced — that was six months ago. I ask Trevor if he consulted Kerrie before he brought his mother into their home and he says, "Yes — and Kerrie said it was fine." In fact, the situation was really no different from the time Kerrie's sister and her daughter came to live with them during the sister's divorce, or the year that Trevor's uncle stayed with them while he was on an extended teaching sabbatical and struggling financially. These things just happened, without much real discussion or planning.

Kerrie and Trevor's marriage does not consist of just the two of them; it's a triangle, with an apex always waiting to be filled with a distraction. When their children were younger, they filled that apex. Since the kids left home, it has been filled by a series of other people with seemingly legitimate reasons for being there, but whose presence also allow Kerrie and Trevor to worry about them, rather than each other. Now Sarah has become that apex.

I express my thoughts about their marriage with Kerrie and Trevor. They agree that open and honest communication has always been a challenge for them and are willing to work on improving it. We spend time each session (and I give them follow-up work for the week) talking about communication and what it means to be an intimate couple. Trevor practices listening to Kerrie voice her thoughts and opinions without interruption, and Kerrie learns to appreciate the fact that her feelings may be different from her husband's.

As Kerrie becomes more confident of her ability to express herself, we also discuss her communication style with her mother-in-law. She is frustrated enough with Sarah that she wants her to leave her home. Yes, she could put her foot down and demand that Trevor find a new home for his mother but there would be consequences to that ultimatum, including her husband's resentment.

Though Kerrie was not completely unjustified in thinking that Sarah was *the* problem in her marriage, therapy revealed that Sarah was only a symptom of a larger issue (lack of open, honest communication). Therapy also allowed Kerrie and Trevor to talk through their feelings and together, build better communication skills for their future as a couple, increasing their tolerance for intimacy along the way.

Acting Out

There's a saying that people either "talk it out" or "act it out." "Acting out" is a term that refers to behavior (sometimes extreme behavior) that is used to express thoughts or feelings the person feels incapable of otherwise expressing directly or in a healthy way. An example might be breaking a lamp rather than saying, "I'm angry with you." The client who is acting out typically falls into one of three categories:

1. The client who does not recognize or admit that he is acting out. He just doesn't see that his "acting out" is simply a distorted and ineffectual way to express his emotions.
2. The client who has an inkling that he is acting out but who wants professional validation and support for doing so.
3. The client who knows he acts out but has been unsuccessful in dealing with it.

In any of these scenarios, I must first determine whether you're in crisis mode (chronic drug or other substance usage, withdrawal or detox, thoughts of suicide, etc.) and whether a higher level of care (hospitalization, intensive outpatient programs, etc.) are needed. Once we have addressed these things, we can proceed with therapy.

If you're seeking therapy for repeated episodes of acting out, chances are you're not the only person in the picture. Other people have quite possibly been hurt, disappointed or angered by your actions. If you're in denial about your behavior but have agreed to therapy for fear of losing someone or something, you may not be ready or willing to change. In the case of addiction, you may not be ready to address the addiction but will at least agree that the relationship at issue is one of extreme importance to you. The fact that you've shown up for therapy underscores that importance. It's my job to help you recognize that your behavior is a pattern, examine both conscious and unconscious motives for engaging in that behavior, and allow you to draw your own conclusions about your actions and the consequences.

Sometimes in this process you discover that old wounds must be healed in order to move past them. Though clients dealing with negative behavior patterns often believe, at least during the initial phase of therapy, that their behavior provides them a much needed “release” or freedom (from feelings, responsibilities, restricted behavior and so on) they soon discover that the behavior actually limits or even imprisons them. When the negative behavior is accepted as something that removes power rather than rewards it, the tide shifts and the healing process begins.

Getting the Most Out of Therapy

I want all of my clients to know that I am there to listen, but to learn and to teach. Though active listening skills are key to success as a therapist, learning and teaching skills are equally valuable. Like any effective teacher, my ultimate goal is to help teach my client how to take care of himself, including new ways at looking at old issues. Sometimes, however there is a period where it’s necessary for me to guide, parent and model for the client until he’s able to stand on his own.

Over the years, I’ve had the privilege of working with some very special people and together we’ve made a great deal of progress toward authoring the story that they want to write. A few, however, truly stand out. They came to my office each week with an open mind and heart, and were honest about their words and actions during the week — even when they knew they had taken a step backwards. They read the books that I suggested (and other books that they came up with on their own), journaled regularly and completed their assignments. Together, we enjoyed a mutually challenging and rewarding relationship. I am telling you this with high hopes that it will inspire you to do the hard work of therapy.

In life, we tend to get out that which we put in, and therapy is no different. For example, let’s say you want to learn more about literature so you enroll in a college course on the subject. You’re excited about the class but soon realize that it requires significant effort, so you decide not to do any of the homework and when the professor lectures, you spend your time texting friends. Would you honestly expect to get anything meaningful out of the experience? Of course not!

Therapy is sort of like taking a college course — only the subject is you. You signed up for the class because you want to know more about you — the parts of yourself that you don't quite understand, or that you haven't yet learned to manage effectively. It's easy to think that because you're paying for therapy (and in most cases, you're not being forced to go), the therapist should be the one to do the heavy lifting. But how would that help you get better?

Preparing for your session is a gift you give to yourself. Spending just a few moments thinking about what has come up during the week, considering your thoughts and behaviors, what you're noticing about yourself, your relationships and the way you are (including certain struggles you're having) is like a stretching exercise before you work out: It helps you grow and prevent repeating the same mistakes that have hurt you numerous times in the past.

Many clients find it helpful to make notes or journal during the week and bring those things with them to their session. Your therapist may or may not actually read them, but you can use them as a reference or topics for discussion during a therapy session. It's also a good idea to jot down any topics left over from your last session that you'd like to continue discussing.

Summing Up

Getting as specific as possible about the reasons you're coming to therapy is the first step in maximizing the therapeutic process. But in the beginning, don't worry if you're not one hundred percent certain of what's bothering you. The fact that you show up each week, ready to talk, means that you're on your way to both feeling and getting better.

CHAPTER 2

WHAT GOES ON IN THE ROOM?

How Does Therapy Work?

We either make ourselves miserable or we make ourselves strong. The amount of work is the same.
— Carlos Castaneda

There's a lot of discussion about why talking with a therapist is considered to be the preferred means of resolving personal problems or interpersonal conflict rather than simply talking things over with a trusted friend, relative or clergy member. After all, before talk therapy came along these were our only choices when it came to giving problems a voice (well, maybe throw in the local bartender or beauty shop stylist) and there's no arguing that even today, talking over problems with them can feel good. But a trained professional offers you five additional and important things:

- Objectivity.
- Confidentiality.
- A deeper understanding of human psychology that will help you discover your own motivations and gain insight about you and your relationship with the world around you.

- Professional education and training to spot emotional or mental problems.
- Professional education and training to help you work towards emotional or mental wellness.

The therapist acts as an expert guide, helping you identify troublesome and challenging areas and behavioral patterns, navigate rough spots, and deal with difficult situations and people.

Talk therapy allows clients to explore thoughts and feelings to better understand how these things affect both mood and behavior. But the goal of therapy is not only to help you unburden your troubles such as anxiety, marital struggles, fears, or loss. It's to help you recognize patterns which, once recognized, will allow you to make positive and healthy change. It's a valuable tool for improving relationship dynamics and interpersonal communication skills. It's also instrumental in helping you realize your full potential and set goals to accomplish dreams and aspirations. It provides relief and professional guidance if you are diagnosed with a clinical disorder. The relationship between the therapist and client is exceptionally important because as it progresses, the relationship may be used as an opportunity to reframe significant emotional experiences and work through them in a safe, nonjudgmental environment.

A recurring theme in this book is an emphasis on recognizing or becoming aware of various thoughts and behaviors which previously were not known to you or not fully recognized by you. This is because a prime virtue of talk therapy is that just talking with a therapist encourages and clarifies recognition or awareness of many previously unknown or unrecognized thoughts and behaviors. It is this increased recognition and awareness that supercharges the therapy process.

Perhaps most importantly, talk therapy promotes the growth of your basic sense of "self" (self-awareness, self-knowledge, self-perception, self-esteem) so that you're better equipped to manage your own thoughts and feelings in a way that maximizes pleasure and minimizes suffering in your daily life.

There's another way of looking at the self through a useful tool called the Johari Window, named for its creators, Joseph Luft and Harry Ingham.[1] The Window looks like Figure 1 below:

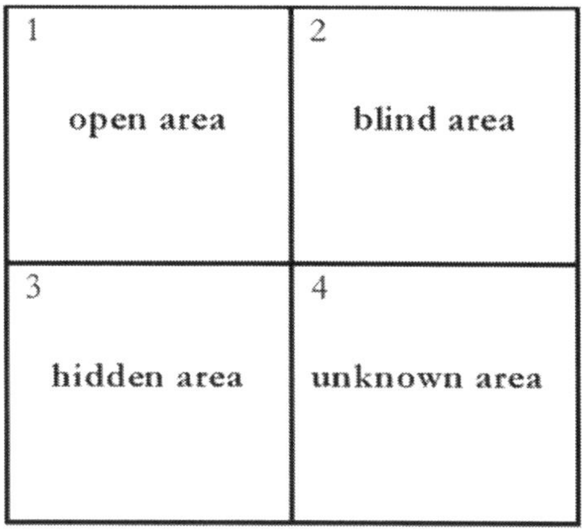

1 **open area**	2 **blind area**
3 **hidden area**	4 **unknown area**

Figure 1

You can see that the Window has four panes, representing the four parts of the self. The *open area* is what you show others about yourself. The *blind area* are those parts of you that others see but you do not. The *hidden area* is what you choose to hide from others. And the *unknown area* includes parts of you that you do not see, nor do others. What happens in therapy is that when I share with you my view of your blind area and you share with me your hidden area, the open area of your life becomes expanded, and the unknown area becomes reduced.

When your basic self is more fully developed, you're naturally more open and genuine with yourself and others. As used in this book, "basic self" refers to a person's "firmest convictions and most integrated beliefs"[2] and which are "solid and non-negotiable with others."[3] In contrast, the "pseudo self" is negotiable with others: "Pseudo-self consists of others' opinions, absorbed as one's own without any personal conscious commitment to the beliefs and convictions underlying the opinions absorbed."[4]

If you have a well-developed basic self, you're also less likely to develop or be restricted by hidden or blind areas because you aren't using them as defenses against things for which you feel shame. The opposite is true for the person whose basic self is less developed.

Therapy can help expand the basic self while reducing blind, hidden and unknown areas, thereby connecting you more fully with your true identity.

Popular Misconceptions

Though the stigma of seeking psychological counseling has dramatically lessened in many social circles over the years, for some people it remains strong. Instead of seeking professional help, they choose to lug around a heavy emotional load for months or even years, tolerating a life that is less than pleasurable because they believe:

- Therapy is only for "crazy" people and I'm not "crazy."
- I should be able to figure this out myself.
- My problem isn't big enough for therapy.
- Therapy takes years before you get better.
- My family/friends would think I'm weak if I saw a therapist.
  Or worse,
- I would think I'm weak if I saw a therapist.

Other reasons that people avoid therapy include having certain personality types (such as those who are emotionally or socially isolated), cultural or religious mores, financial/health insurance constraints and/or the belief that "I'd rather just take a pill." Though some of these issues go beyond the limits of my profession, I would like to take a look at some commons misconceptions and nip them in the bud. Now that you're *Ready to Talk*, I don't want anything standing in your way.

Misconception #1: Therapy is for crazy people.

Of course, this isn't true. Therapy provides a safe and non-judgmental environment and process for voicing your problems, concerns and worries in private with an objective person who is educated and experienced in dealing with these problems. It was only a generation or so ago that it was mostly "crazy" or highly neurotic people who sought therapy. These days, therapists often work with the "walking wounded" — people who are functioning adequately in their lives but who want to improve the quality of their lives and live a healthier, more meaningful life. I also see a good number of clients who have what is called an "adjustment disorder". They're simply having difficulty adjusting to life's ups and downs. They're depressed and/or anxious and though they don't meet a clinical description (i.e., a formal diagnosis) of depression or anxiety, for example, they're having a tough time coping and need new tools to be able to do so. How crazy is that?

Misconception #2: I should be able to figure this out myself.

My guess is that you're an intelligent person who figures things out for yourself all the time. But something is bugging you and so far, you *haven't* been able to figure it out on your own. It isn't because you're dumb or lazy but because you cannot be objective and impartial about yourself.

Misconception #3: My problem isn't big enough for therapy.

But it's *bothering* you! And they're your feelings — and, by the way, your feelings are a perfectly good enough reason to seek therapy.

Misconception #4: My family/friends would think I'm weak if I saw a therapist.

First of all, no one but you needs to know you're seeing a therapist, unless of course you choose to tell someone. Therapists honor the confidentiality of the identity of their clients as well as the content of what they say in therapy. Will anyone think you're weak for taking charge of your own happiness? Added point about therapy if you have this misconception: If you're that concerned about what others think of you, therapy is the right place for you.

Misconception #5: I would think I'm weak if I saw a therapist.
See response to Misconception #4.

Misconception #6: Therapy takes years before you get better.
Therapy is a highly individualized process and it really depends on both the nature of the problem(s) and you. While deep-seated issues typically do take longer to unravel and resolve, therapy can also be a useful and quick tool for developing better communication skills and improving interpersonal relationships. Ultimately, however, efficiency is most significantly enhanced when you're open, honest and willing to do the work necessary for improvement.

Unfortunately, some people delay seeking help for so long that by the time they reach my office, they're in crisis mode and may even require comprehensive care. The good news is that once their emotions are stabilized, they can begin the process of unloading their burdens and often find immediate relief. The simple act of sharing your problem with another person trained to assist in the best possible way proves to be highly cathartic. However (and you will hear me repeat this), *feeling* better is not the same as *getting* better. The latter takes time, effort and patience.

Why Do We Avoid Talking?

So, what is it about sharing your problems that can seem so scary or overwhelming? I think it's partly because many family systems (the home and family environment in which we're raised) teach us to avoid discussion of important personal issues. If you don't grow up witnessing first-hand examples of problem sharing and solving or discussions about acceptance and change, you're unlikely to suddenly wake up one day with that knowledge implanted in your brain. To be sure, life is a winding path that's planted with joy and littered with pain. Along the way, you'll inevitably encounter harsh difficulties and experience unpleasant feelings — both are integral parts of the life experience in its entirety. However, if you've been taught to go *around* problems instead of face them head on, you'll inevitably pick up other problems along the way. For example, rather than risking vulnerability by calling a friend when you feel helpless or sad, you may pour a glass or two of wine to lessen your worry. Or instead of speaking up when your spouse criticizes your spending habits, instead of speaking up, you go shopping to show him what *real* spending is all about. But it's this type of action (or, *acting out*) that prevents you from living your truth and that fuels distorted thinking.

In fact, most addictions and destructive behavior patterns stem from looking at a "bad" situation and deciding to avert your gaze. Relieving fear with a distraction may provide some temporary relief from dealing with the root of the problem, at least for a while, but the price for doing so can be high.

How Therapy Has Evolved

If you're a fan of the popular television series *Mad Men* — about cocktail-swilling, chain-smoking advertising executives in 1960's Manhattan — you've probably seen the episodes where the main character's wife, Betty Draper, puffs nervously away on cigarettes in a darkened room while reclining on the proverbial psychoanalyst's couch (as much as one *can* recline on a sterile, mid-century designed leather slab). She talks to her silent doctor seated behind her, the only other sound in the room the scratch of his pen on a notepad. Betty starts the conversation (really, a monologue with a title) out of nowhere:

"Thanksgiving."

She continues along, freely associating and switching randomly between topics, from small struggles like getting everyone together for the holiday to much larger concerns such as how she might be permitting her husband's continual cheating. Though she admits she feels better "just talking about her problems," most therapy today is not done this way, with little feedback from or interaction with the therapist) will ultimately lead to a meaningful or inspirational relationship between them. Watching the scene makes me appreciate how much the therapeutic process has evolved over the past forty or so years.

Who Does the Talking?

Some clients are more talkative than others. And that's just fine with me. Others are plenty talkative but prefer that I start the session with a few leading questions. It really doesn't matter who starts the conversation or what we discuss, so long as we're talking and our topics are beneficial to you. Some days, those topics might be light-hearted and humorous; others, much deeper — perhaps even tearful and painful; and others, joyous and insightful.

Depending on the client's personality and the particular day, I act interchangeably as friend, parent, confidante and sounding board. We might use various techniques such as role-playing, if that's something that's helpful to him, allowing him to hear himself process through anticipated difficult encounters or bolster his confidence in relationships.

The same is true for couple's or family counseling. One person may be talking to another while I observe, or one person may be addressing an issue with me while the other person (or people) observe. When the latter scenario takes place, the observing person gains the benefit of a more objective vantage point (almost as if viewing a conversation between actors on a stage). My particular therapeutic style is fairly active and educational. Other therapists may employ a more passive role, choosing instead to interrupt infrequently during the session.

I typically have a few ideas regarding what we might talk about during a session, but it really depends on the client's preference, needs and current circumstances of his life. Some clients want me to bring up topics of discussion and I can certainly do that. I often begin a session with a follow-up from the previous session; this might be discussing any of your thoughts and feelings from what we previously talked about or perhaps reviewing homework assignments. Sometimes we simply continue the conversation from the last session. This feels something like turning to a dog-eared page of a book we put down a week ago.

But generally I believe it's more productive for the client to determine what he needs to talk about. This is particularly true if he has unresolved feelings from his last session or about something that occurred since our last session. If he's angry or upset with me, or he had a dream about me (which is quite common for clients to dream about their therapists), or he has been hesitant to ask my opinion on something, it's a good idea for him to share these feelings at the beginning of the session so that they're less likely to impact the remainder of it.

If you're feeling uncertain about what to talk about in a therapy session, one simple way to get inspiration is to recount to me events that have occurred since the last session, then explore your thoughts and feelings about one or more of these events.

Some clients also benefit by bringing their journal to our sessions and we discuss it together, using a collaborative approach for working through a situation. We'll talk more about journaling in Chapter Seven.

Is It Just Talking?

No, it is also very much about thinking. Thinking is critical not just in life but also in the therapy room. I'm talking about deep, profound thinking about relationships, values, beliefs, goals, behavior and preferences. It's also about education.

However, often when clients first come to therapy they're in such emotional distress (for instance, they've just learned their spouse has been cheating or that their child has been doing drugs), before we can get to working with thinking and education, I need to help them work through the intense feelings around the situation that brought them to therapy.

Once the client has learned to handle his emotions better, we can move on to thinking and education. You may be wondering what I mean by thinking. I will address this in more detail in future chapters, but it includes things like helping the client come to understand his core beliefs, understand his distorted thinking patterns and deeply thinking about his values.

As a therapist a lot of time educating my clients on various topics that might apply to their circumstances. Topics may include symptoms of ADD, anxiety or depression; communication styles; or sibling birth order and how that might play a role in the client's life. I may give them handouts or encourage them to read specific books or articles, or to watch a TED talk. And whenever possible and appropriate, I give them the opportunity to work on learning to balance their thoughts and feelings.

Do I Have to Talk About My Family?

Most client-therapist relationships begin with you, the client, presenting your problems or concerns to me, the therapist. But even if you tell me something very personal and intimate about yourself in the first few sessions, I still don't yet know you intimately. I'm able to draw certain conclusions about why you might be suffering or how therapy will be beneficial to you, but to really understand what you're all about, I need to know something about where you're coming from and your background. Yes, at some point I'm probably going to ask you about your family and your upbringing.

This typically occurs during the second or third session but if appropriate can happen during the very first session. However, if you're in crisis mode, we're less likely to focus initially on family dynamics and instead the session may be more about managing anxiety, breathing and meditation techniques and other types of self-soothing techniques.

It's not unusual for a client to ask why it's necessary for me to know about their parents, siblings, school years, childhood activities and the like. They may say something like, "I'm here because I drink too much or have anxiety, or am depressed or unfulfilled. What does that have to do with my childhood?" It's a legitimate question and one that, to be answered correctly, requires an understanding of how family systems work. Don't skip over this next brief section. It pertains to you, too.

The *family genogram* is a little drawing that uses symbols to represent a person's family relationships and history, identifying patterns and psychological factors that influence those relationships. It's basically a family tree that also shows life transitions (such as marriage, birth, death, etc.) and helps identify patterns of behavior and illness such as alcoholism, obesity and child abuse. It allows the therapist to get to know you and what you come from.

When used to represent your family, the symbols have the capability of carrying golden nuggets of useful information — things that help me get to know you better, but also aid you in identifying how relationships have affected you for better or worse, including your behavioral patterns and health risks (both physical and mental). Understanding an individual's feelings and behavior as part of a family system has been compared to seeing the positions of as many players as possible on the field at the same time.

For example, through a genogram I might learn that depression or abuse is common in your family; women in your family tend to marry passive, unhappy, unsuccessful men; anxiety is prevalent; that at least one person from the previous three generations has "cut off" from the family. See Figure 2 and Figure 3 below[5] for some common genogram symbols and an example of a genogram.

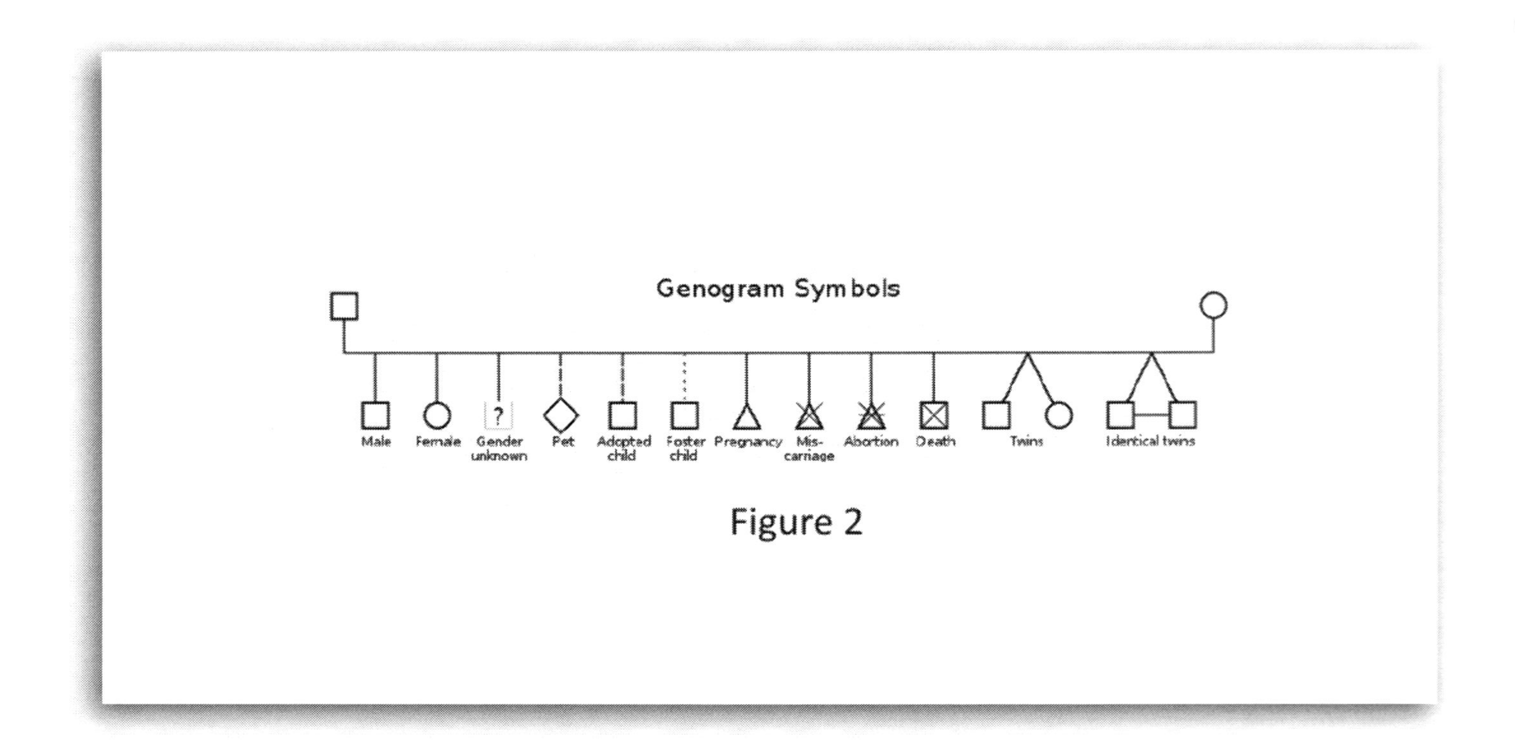
Genogram Symbols
?
Male
Female
Gender unknown
Pet
Adopted child
Foster child
Pregnancy
Mis-carriage
Abortion
Death
Twins
Identical twins

Figure 2

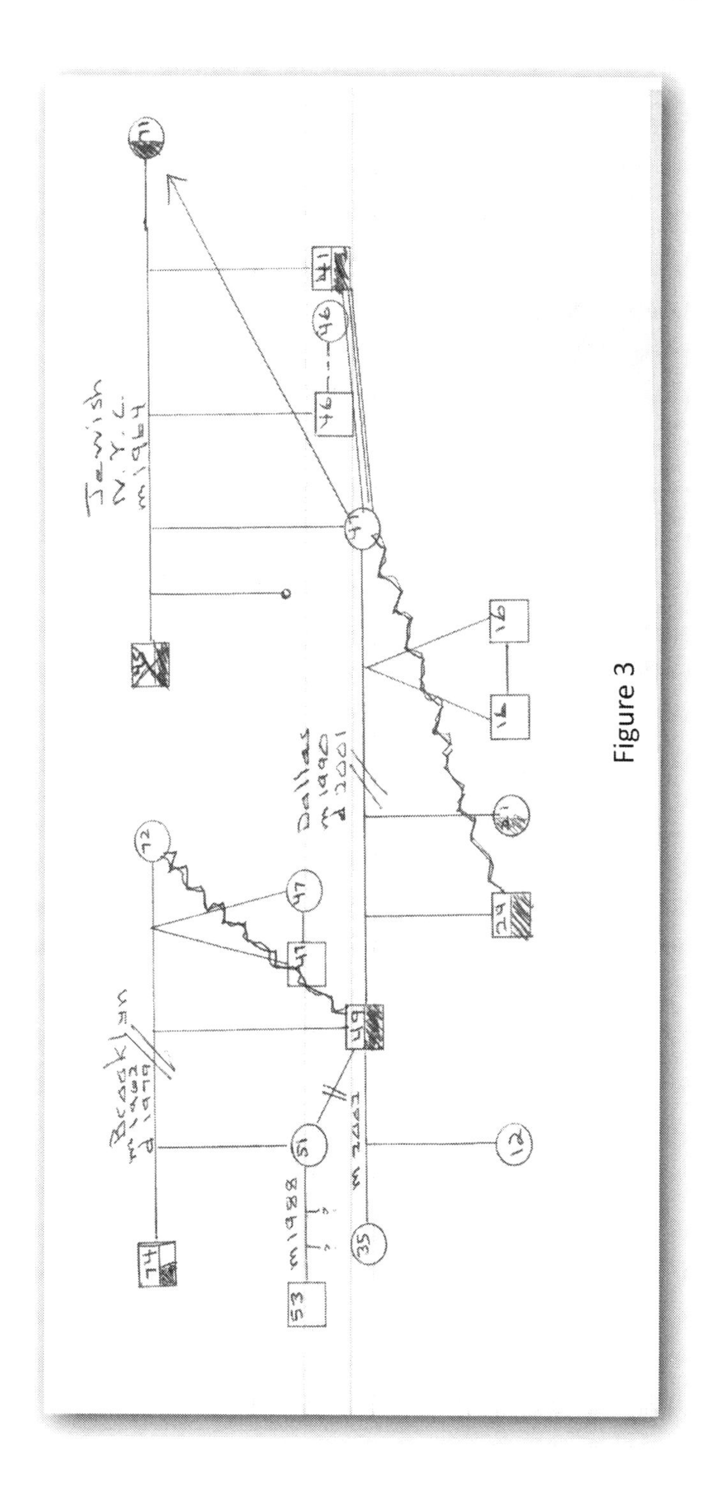

Figure 3

Workout

In a journal or notebook, draw a simple genogram of your own family, starting with yourself at the bottom center. To get started, find a free genogram template online. Include any siblings next to you, then work upwards to include your parents, grandparents, aunts and uncles, and so on. Note any significant life transitions (marriages, births, illnesses, deaths of love ones, etc.) for each individual, using either one of the genogram symbols on the previous page or by simply writing it in. Do you begin to see relationship patterns? Health patterns? What can you learn from your own family's history? Here are some questions to consider: What was your role in the family system? What messages about gender were communicated? How was anger expressed? How was love communicated? What was your parents' relationship like and how have your relationships been similar or different? How did your family handle transitions or crisis?

A Note on Confidentiality

Confidentiality between client and therapist is of utmost importance. It is both legally and ethically required of therapists. Importantly, confidentiality also encourages and ensures open communication between client and therapist. The Health Insurance Portability and Accountability Act (HIPAA) established national standards to protect an individual's medical records and other personal health information. After Betty Draper of *Mad Men* meets with her psychiatrist, her husband Don sneaks into a quiet room of their home and calls up the good doc, who is more than willing to spill the beans on everything Betty has told him that afternoon in session. Yet another reason to be thankful we've moved past the '60's! (That, and bouffant hairdos).

For the record, *everything* that you tell your therapist during session is considered confidential, unless he thinks (or you say) you're suicidal, homicidal or there is reason to believe there is child/elder/mental retardation abuse going on in your life. One of the papers you will sign when we first meet is a confidentiality agreement, which sets for the scope and limits of confidentiality. You also may choose to sign a consent form that allows your therapist to consult another professional (who is probably also bound by confidentiality) such as a medical doctor or psychiatrist if deemed necessary, or perhaps other selected individuals you or I may suggest. And even with your signed consent form, the subjects that can be discussed are limited to those approved by you and you can revoke your consent at any time.

In my own therapy practice, we use what is called a collaborative approach, which means that all our therapists meet weekly to discuss and collaborate on all our clients' therapeutic processes. Our clients benefit not only from the education, training, skills and experience of their therapist — they also benefit from the synergy of the entire group. Because of this, our clients also sign a consent form that allows this peer consultation, but all our therapists are all bound by confidentiality.

How Does a Session Typically End?

Just as the beginning of the session depends on the particular client, so, too is when therapy ends. At the end of the first or second session, as I'm getting to know you, I typically end with a summary of what you've shared and a plan for moving forward. I'll say something like, "Here are the things that I'm hearing that I think we need to explore…". These topics may include communication, growing a basic self and/or growing up, managing anxieties and learning self-soothing techniques, dealing with relationships, infidelity, betrayal and so on.

How Many Sessions Does It Typically Take?

Without intending to sound frivolous, successful therapy takes as many sessions as it takes. That is to say, the healing process requires adequate time to develop a relationship with your therapist so that he knows you well enough to help you. And just like any other relationship, familiarity is sometimes established quickly and sometimes it isn't. It really depends on the personalities of both client and therapist, how open the client is to sharing personal information and how much work he is willing to put into the process between sessions. Just because a therapist is a trained professional, theoretically adept at reading people, doesn't mean that he will know you very well after just a few sessions. The relationship with your therapist is potentially one of the most significant you will have in your lifetime; give it the time it deserves to develop and enrich.

It's common for clients who have worked through major issues and have "completed" therapy to come back periodically to consult with me on a current concern. I also recommend to my clients that they come in regularly for a check-up just as they do for a physical check-up with their primary physician, once a year or so.

Summing Up

Your therapeutic experience should be as individual as you are, taking into account your personality, comfort levels, family of origin and both short and long-term goals. Each person goes on a different journey toward knowing himself better. As you become more familiar with the therapeutic process, you'll become more confident in the specific ways that it can help you.

CHAPTER 3

WHAT ARE THE GOALS OF THERAPY?

Feeling Better vs. Getting Better

To find out what is truly individual in ourselves, profound reflection is needed; and suddenly we realize how uncommonly difficult the discovery of individuality in fact is.
— Carl Jung

Do not follow where the path may lead.
Go instead where there is no path and leave a trail.
— Harold R. McAlindon

When you begin therapy, the immediate goal is to simply feel better, right? You're hurting and you want someone to help you figure out how to stop the pain. Remember, though, *feeling better* is not the same as *getting better*. The ultimate goal of therapy, then, is to *get* better. But how do you do that? What are the steps that take you in the direction of getting better?

The answer varies for everyone, and so does the therapeutic process. Some therapy is very solution-focused, designed, for example, to assist someone in the grieving process, or help develop strategies to overcome a relationship obstacle or a stalled career. Other therapy is geared more toward cleaning up the wreckage of the past and healing the inner child. Still other therapy is a combination of these two types and includes discovering how past relationships and situations affect present and future relationships. The last example is typical of the type of therapy that I practice, involving individuals, couples or families seeking solutions in order to create new and healthier perspectives within themselves and in their relationships.

Before you can more fully develop your relationships with others, you must first do so with yourself. You need a clearer picture of who you really are including your core values, vital needs, goals and dreams. It's only in this understanding of your basic self that you can truly *get better*.

The Basic Self Defined

Each and every one of us is unique. Your individual identity is based on numerous factors such as genetics, environmental conditions, family of origin, likes, preferences and passions, to name a few. This core identity is known as the "basic self." It has been called the answer to the age-old question, "Who Am I?" But in our lifelong attempt to answer that question in an authentic way, we sometimes become entangled with obstacles; instead of remaining true to what makes us happy and productive, we succumb to our own self-limiting beliefs, distorted thinking and other people's opinions — and it leaves us feeling out of sorts.

Noted American psychiatrist Murray Bowen developed a family systems theory, sometimes called the Bowen Theory, of the basic self and how it relates to others, particularly those within the same family system. According to Bowen, "[p]eople with better levels of differentiation (defined and further discussed in Chapter Five) are more contained people, they're more sure of themselves and clearer about the responsibility of self and responsibility to each other, and important family decisions are based more on the reality of the situation than on the emotion of the moment."[6]

Other people's opinions do serve a useful purpose. Feedback from peers and loved ones is an essential component of being human, keeping you balanced, focused and more open-minded to the possibility of change. But when you sacrifice your own values, desires and needs to please someone else, you get into trouble. We begin to lose our basic self, and watch seemingly helplessly as it diminishes before our eyes.

Take a look at Figure 4, which depicts how the basic self interacts with the world around it.

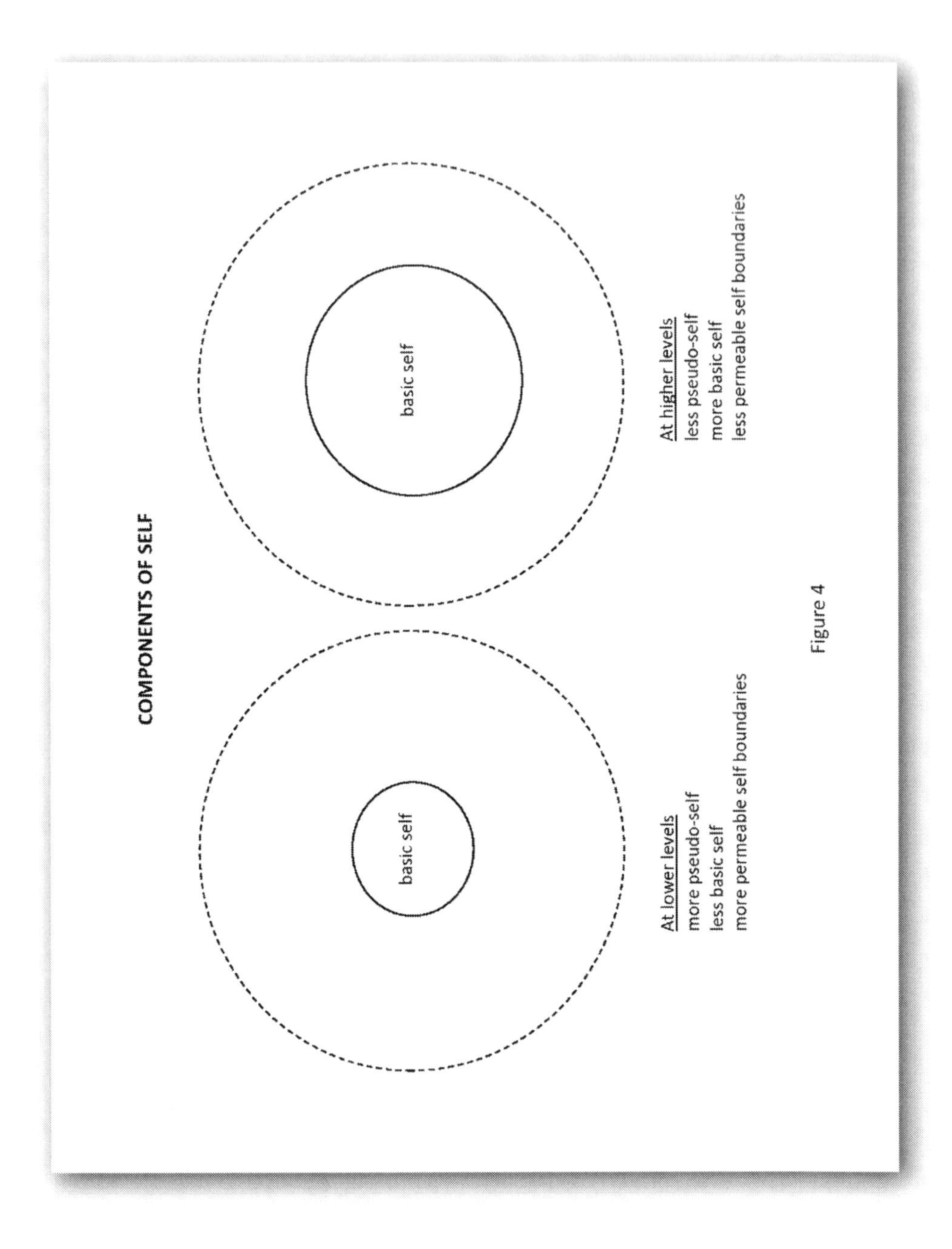
COMPONENTS OF SELF
basic self
At lower levels
more pseudo-self
less basic self
more permeable self boundaries
basic self
At higher levels
less pseudo-self
more basic self
less permeable self boundaries

Figure 4

In the center of the circle on the left is the basic self, which we previously defined as "a person's firmest convictions and most integrated beliefs"[7] and which are "solid and non-negotiable with others." [8]It's quite small in comparison to the larger circle that surrounds it (the area labeled "pseudo-self", which we previously defined as consisting of "others' opinions, absorbed as one's own without any personal conscious commitment to the beliefs and convictions underlying the opinions absorbed"[9] and which are negotiable with others. When the basic self is not adequately developed or established, the pseudo-self fills up with external junk.

Now look at the circle on the right. When the basic self is larger, there is less room for a pseudo-self. As the basic self enlarges, you don't have the need to define self through "others' opinions, beliefs and convictions." In consequence, you have more balance in your life, you have healthier relationships, there is less chaos in your life, you are better able to manage anxieties, and you are a healthier, happier and more emotionally stable person.

This leads us to our first goal in therapy:

Goal #1: Enlarge the Basic Self

Though talk therapy naturally involves plenty of talking, it's not only this cathartic act that heals your pain. If my client Lisa tells me that her father is controlling and very angry, it may initially bring her relief (especially because it's something she has never felt comfortable discussing, especially with her own family) but it will not solve the problem of how she can learn to deal with his aggressive traits. She cannot change her father, she can only reduce his hold over her by managing her reactions to him and to do this, she must first enlarge her basic sense of self. When she learns to rely on her own judgment and value her own opinions, she will become significantly less concerned by her father's behavior toward her.

Other goals in therapy include:

Goal #2: Get Comfortable with Risk Taking

One of the many benefits of enlarging the basic self is a reduced emphasis on what others say and think (or what you *think* they think) and from this develops a wonderful opportunity for growth: risk taking.

Life is full of uncertainty but if your life is going to truly feel and get better, you're going to have to get comfortable with the notion of taking risks. I've always loved this question: *What would you do if you knew you could not fail?* Perhaps an even better question is: *What would you do if you believed it was okay to fail?*

Consider this quote by Helen Keller, a woman who knew a great deal about taking risks:

> *Security is mostly a superstition. It does not exist in nature, nor do the children of men as a whole experience it. Avoiding danger is no safer in the long run than outright exposure. Life is either a daring adventure or nothing.*

Keller believed that without risks, life is less meaningful, less satisfying, and that avoiding risk doesn't really keep us protected. However, taking risks means putting yourself out there; making yourself vulnerable to the world and its sometimes harsh judgments yet staying true to yourself. How can you possibly engage in risk, and therefore in growth, when you're paralyzed with worry about what others think?

I want to mention here that it's not necessarily what people actually *do* think of you. Unless they tell you in specific terms, you're just speculating or, worse, assuming. Spending your precious time trying to somehow worm your way into other people's thoughts, feelings and opinions. Noted author and speaker Wayne Dyer said it best: "What other people think of me is none of my business." And I would add to that, "Until they make it my business by telling me." Until then, you're only speculating.

Taking risks is not just about going after that big promotion you've worked so hard for, or finding your way out of a bad but familiar relationship — although those are both good examples. Risk also has a lot to do with giving up long-held beliefs about yourself and others, in seeing relationships for what they really are, and deciding on your own terms whether you want to continue participating in them.

Goal #3: Clarify Distorted Thinking

As a therapist, I frequently witness numerous versions of distorted thinking. Though each of has only one brain, we're able to use it to create a dual version of ourselves — the one that is our basic self and the one that we project to others.

At its base level, distorted thinking is really a defense mechanism; something you use to protect ourselves when you:

1. Believe you're not lovable just as you really are — *It's not that he's such a bad husband even though he abuses me. I should really be a better wife.*
2. Engage in self-loathing — *I probably shouldn't ask for a raise. I don't really deserve a bigger salary.*
3. Practice self-fulfilling prophesies — *I may as well eat unhealthy foods and not take care of myself. Everyone in my family has heart disease anyway.*
4. Fail to commit to your personal growth —. *I may say I want to get better but I'm really not willing to do the actual work to make it happen.*
5. Make excuses or blame others for your mistakes because it's easier than taking responsibility for them. *It's not my fault I forgot to pick you up for the meeting; you should have called and reminded me.*

In talk therapy, you learn to process through distorted thinking — first, by learning to recognize when you're doing it; and second, substituting distorted thinking with clearer thoughts of who you really are but without judging yourself.

Goal #4: Rewrite Your Story

When I talk about rewriting your story through therapy, it doesn't mean that you should erase your past and go about your life pretending the past never happened. Though there may have been challenging, disappointing, confusing or painful events in your past, they're part of who you are today. You can't change that. But what you *can* change is how you relate to your past.

Rather than focusing your energy on the hurts of your past, you can redirect it for better use. You may use pain to enhance compassion for others going through a similar experience. Or you may use it as a way to help raise awareness to tragic situations so that others learn from them. You can use your past to help make you stronger or more determined.

By reframing the context of your past, and by that I mean changing your emotional experience of the past facts and events, it informs your current life; it doesn't define it. Your past becomes a memory that helps you move forward. Reframing gives you a different perspective, encouraging growth in new directions — helping you write new and better chapters, and stripping away the harsh judgment that often accompanies an underdeveloped basic self.

Goal #5: Manage Your Feelings

When a person has a well-developed basic self and is adequately differentiated from those around him, he is far more likely to react in a calmer, more thoughtful manner when exposed to potentially stressful events. He realizes that he is an autonomous creature, but also one who is drawn toward connections with others. This person is confident in his decision making abilities and therefore, not at the mercy of his partner, family or the groups in which he is engaged. Nor is he at the mercy of their emotions.

This is not to say he's a robot. Feelings are natural and automatic responses to life circumstances. You will never be able to prevent feeling — why would you even want to? But the person who is able to manage his feelings will inevitably experience a more pleasurable, less anxiety-filled existence. We'll talk more about this in the Chapter Four.

Mastering these goals through time, practice and patience ultimately leads to a higher level of differentiation including less anxiety and mutually fulfilling relationships. But there is another important goal in therapy and that includes changing the way you think or, in other words, changing the brain.

Goal #6: Changing the Brain

Researchers James Prochaska and Carlo DiClemente and created a model regarding effective change that involves six necessary steps.[10] The model indicates an individual's levels of readiness and commitment and provide a sort of roadmap for therapy. They are:

- Precontemplation – not even thinking there is a problem or need for change.
- Contemplation – willingness to consider the possibility of a problem or need for change.
- Determination – Making a commitment to action; being ready to change.
- Action – Putting a plan into action.
- Maintenance – Firmly establishing the new plan; dealing with relapses toward old behavior.
- Termination – Old behavior or problem ceases.

Habitual action lays down neural pathways in our brains that influence or even govern our future behavior. Thus you've been doing and thinking a certain way for so long that your emotions are often just kneejerk reactions as if you are on autopilot. By learning to manage emotions, you're actually rewiring these neural pathways. The good news is that your brain, a living organ, is capable of being reshaped. But the only way to do that is to do things differently, creating new neural pathways. This is part of what therapy is about.

There's a good deal of contemporary literature suggesting just how many days it takes to create a new habit; some experts say twenty-one days while others insist it's more like ninety. Either way, there is truth to the idea that new habits require repetition. If you have a depressed brain and do nothing, you'll continue to have a depressed brain. When you intervene (perhaps with talk therapy, medications, consciously changing thought patterns, etc.), you start producing a non-depressed brain.

Measuring Improvement in Therapy

Therapy, like anything else from which you wish to gain benefit, requires identifying clear goals, breaking down seemingly insurmountable tasks into small, manageable steps and checking back frequently to see how you're doing. Consider this quote from John E. Jones: "What gets measured gets done, what gets measured and fed back gets done well, what gets rewarded gets repeated." *This* is how you overcome difficulties — by replacing negative behavior patterns with healthier ones and eventually emerging as the successful author of your own life story. But in my experience as a therapist, it's often the "small victories" that bring the greatest joy because those are the obstacles that trip us up on a daily basis, often leading to much larger problems.

Danae is a soft-spoken woman in her early forties, recently separated, without children and wondering how she'll start over without her husband at her side. She is employed as an accounts administrator at an assisted living home for the elderly. Though she first came to me because she was struggling with how to tell her spouse she didn't want to be married to him anymore, several other things came up during our first few sessions.

Danae has a lifelong obsession with pleasing others, the "disease to please" as she calls it. I think she has aptly named her condition, as the word "disease" is commonly defined as something that impairs normal functioning and is manifested by physical symptoms. In Danae's case, those symptoms included frequent bouts of insomnia, chronic digestion problems and migraine headaches. She is unsure how or when she developed her condition. She had a fairly happy childhood, she tells me, with parents who loved her and four older siblings she adored.

As we explore together the details of her childhood, I learn that there is a significant age gap between Danae and her next eldest sister — eleven years, to be exact. She spent a great deal of her formative years yearning to be just like her siblings. And as an intelligent little girl, she learned quickly that the fastest way to gain acceptance by her cool, much older family members was to try to act just like them.

When she was with her sister Jane, she was an outdoorsy tomboy who loved riding bikes, hiking and playing volleyball. With brother Dylan, she was a voracious reader, shy and quiet. With brother Jordan, she was a prankster with a wild sense of humor and highly theatrical. And with oldest sister Anne, she was mature, responsible and always looking for ways to take care of (and sometimes control) others. So which one was the real Danae? Answer: Sadly, she is none of them. Though there are some elements of her siblings in Danae's personality, she also has her own unique traits that she kept hidden from them in order to get them (or so she believed) to love her.

Have you ever seen the Woody Allen movie *Zelig*? In this 1983 mockumentary, Allen plays Leonard Zelig, a character who so desperately seeks approval that he takes on not only other people's personality traits but also some of their physical characteristics. When he is with a group of Chicago gangsters at a 1920's speakeasy, he wears a pinstriped zoot suit, drinks bathtub gin and plans shootouts. At the very same party, he morphs into an African American jazz musician, blowing on a trumpet as passionately as Louis Armstrong.

Though Danae did not take her people pleasing tendencies to such comedic extremes as Zelig, she spent many years trying to be someone else. She had never really asked herself what she wanted, and what she liked doing — and what she didn't. It wasn't terribly surprising that at 42, she felt as though she still didn't know what she wanted to be when she "grew up" and that her thoughts and opinions didn't really matter.

Also not surprising is that since she was 23, she has been married to a man who does everything for her. From filling up her car with gas every week to scheduling her dental appointments to making dinner every night, Rick was the main breadwinner, decision maker and Danae's full-time caretaker. All she really had to do was show up to work on time, do her job and drive herself home. Rick even packed her lunch and cashed her paychecks for her. He liked golf, so she played golf. He liked Tex-Mex food so that's what they ate most of the time. Rick was an avid collector of antique clown figurines, so those become Danae's hobby, too.

Identifying Clear Goals

Early in our relationship, Danae and I sat down with pen and paper and talked about the goals she wanted to accomplish in therapy. Her main goal was to summon up the courage to tell her husband she wanted a divorce. That's undeniably a big one. But there were several other "smaller" goals linked to it: She also wanted to learn how to speak up for herself including asking for a long overdue raise, discover her own passions and figure out whether she wanted to make a career change. Each of these goals was significant in and of itself so we started with those first.

Baby Steps

If you tell me you want to be a writer but have never written a published piece, I wouldn't say, "Start with a 300-page novel; it's easy." Instead, I may suggest you try sitting down every day for a month and writing something, *anything*, for thirty minutes to see whether it's something you actually enjoy. The same is true if you have always dreamed of running a marathon but you've never exercised more than ten minutes at a time. You start with baby steps, achieving small measures of success that will boost your confidence in yourself and your abilities and keep going from there.

Danae's First Step: Learning how to speak up for herself.

Every morning on her way to work, Danae stopped at a local mom and pop coffee shop for a cappuccino and a toasted bagel with cream cheese (by the way, this breakfast combination is the same one her husband always ordered). She'd grown quite fond of the couple who owned the shop and enjoyed chatting with them for a few minutes before heading to her office. The only problem was, one or both of the owners often got her order wrong. The large-sized coffee she always requested was often delivered as a small or medium; the bagel was sometimes untoasted or the wrong flavor and they occasionally forgot the cream cheese.

For some people, small errors like these might be laughed off or no big deal but for Danae, it was a steady source of disappointment. And even more disappointing to her was her frequent decision to say nothing about it. When I asked her why she remained silent with an order she was unhappy about, she said, "It shouldn't upset me, right? I mean, there are worse problems in the world." While I agreed that there are indeed worse problems, I reminded Danae that these things actually did bother her. Could she, the next time it happened, say, "My order is not correct; will you please fix it for me?" She said that she could. Luckily, the spotty attention to detail at her favorite coffee shop gave Danae plenty of opportunities to ask for what she *really* wanted. Soon, she was ready to practice her new skill in other areas.

Danae's Second Step: Discovering her own passions.

If you've been borrowing your hobbies, interests and ideas from other people, it's time to take a break and focus on what really gets you going.

Danae knew that she loved reading but tended to stick with books that her husband deemed worthy: science fiction and biographies of American political figures. Nothing wrong with either of these genres but Danae actually preferred romantic fiction. It was easy enough for her to find a few books that suited her own tastes — browsing on websites like Amazon or GoodReads couldn't be simpler.

Danae had come to actually enjoy playing golf, even if it was originally her husband's favorite game — she just didn't necessarily enjoy playing with him because he was often critical of her skills. She booked a few rounds by herself and ending up joining as a fourth player to a fun group of women with whom she has become friendly.

Danae's Third Step: Figuring out what's next.

This goal is easy for some people and incredibly difficult for others. There's no right or wrong answer regarding how long it takes to reach this goal. With my clients, I'm more focused *not* on the length of time but in the progress made toward achieving it.

Danae came to me with a need to discuss marital problems and figure out a way to end her relationship. But by focusing on smaller, more manageable tasks like speaking up for herself and discovering her own passions, something interesting happened along the way: She became less emotionally dependent on her husband, found more joy in her daily activities, was less critical of herself and began to respect her own opinions and needs. For the time being, she and her husband are separated and she's spending some time by herself sorting things out. Whether her marriage will survive, I don't yet know but Danae is in a good place and looking forward to her next chapter.

Workout

In your journal, write down what you want for your life in one year, five years, ten years and so on. Think about relationships, children, education, careers, achievements, legacies? Perhaps it's to be less angry, anxious or depressed? What do you want to keep and what do you want to let go of?

Summing Up

One of the questions I ask new clients via a written questionnaire is what brings them to therapy and what are their goals of therapy. I often refer back to those statements as a reminder to myself and to the client of their therapeutic goals.

The simple act of writing down your goals doubles your likelihood for achieving them. This is yet another reason why keeping a journal is so important to the therapeutic process. If you believe that you have strayed from your original goals(s), make a note to discuss it with your therapist at your next session.

Additional Reps

Think about three things that you have learned about yourself since beginning therapy. Try not to judge them as good or bad things; they're just things you didn't before realize. Perhaps you now know that you're more creative than you originally thought, or that punctuality and organization are very important to you. You may have discovered that you rage just like your father rather than express underlying feelings of pain. Write these down in your journal. It's important to acknowledge change, success and growth toward the achievement of your goals.

CHAPTER 4

THOUGHTS AND FEELINGS

What's the Difference?

A little kingdom I possess
Where thoughts and feelings dwell;
And very hard the task I find
Of governing it well.
— Louisa May Alcott, excerpt from *My Kingdom*

Somehow the word "thoughts" has often become interchangeable with the word "feelings". Have you ever considered how you and others interchange these two words? They're not the same. You feel feelings and you think thoughts but our language often confuses the two. Consider the following:

Your boss tells you, "I feel we need to focus more on quality control."

A friend says, "I think I'm sad because my husband plays golf without me."

A politician states, "Let me tell you how I feel about global warming: It's devastating our planet."

It's no wonder that so many of us live in daily confusion about our feelings. It's too bad that we aren't given some sort of written guide when we're old enough to understand that we *feel* feelings, we think thoughts, and they're both an integral part of our life experience. They're neither good nor bad; they just are.

When I use the word "feeling" I'm not talking about physical feelings ("I feel tired", "I feel a pain in my leg", "I feel sunburned".) I'm talking about emotions. (Some people make a distinction between feelings and emotions, but for the purposes of this book I'll use them interchangeably.)

The sometimes-mixed messages received about feelings depends largely on your family of origin. In some households, feelings are acknowledged and dealt with in a healthy and appropriate manner. But in others they can be a source of shame, or portrayed as "a lack of intellect or control," or are "disrespectful" and "self-centered." You may have been ridiculed, minimized and shunned for your feelings. Isn't it interesting that you're taught to feel shame about shame? Or anger about anger?

Thoughts reflect your beliefs, ideas and opinions and they're potentially powerful precursors to your actions. They can be changed based on whatever information you have available at any given time. With practice, you can learn to stop a negative thought by recognizing when you're engaging in this practice and replacing it with a more positive alternative. You can also postpone thoughts by engaging in a physical or mental activity that you enjoy.

Feelings, however, are more difficult to change. Have you ever felt anger or guilt toward something or someone and told yourself, "I shouldn't feel that way. I must be a bad person. I'll try to change." It rarely works, right? That's because feelings are automatic, involuntary experiences. To blame or judge ourselves for something that is an automatic, involuntary experience creates shame or other damaging results. Feelings also give you helpful information that can guide you in making decisions about how to interact with the world around you. Feelings are constantly changing. They're like waves of the ocean; until you "do something about them," (acknowledge, name them, process or act on them) they keep rolling in and out, moment after moment. Sometimes they're gentle but consistent; other times, they're overwhelming, with a tsunami-like force.

If we don't directly acknowledge and process them, feelings will nonetheless be expressed or experienced in other ways, such as physical health issues, passive-aggressive behavior, distorted thinking, or explosive anger. Check out the rapidly growing number of medical studies posted on the Internet, warning us of the physical effects of long-term unexpressed emotion. Heart disease, digestive disorders and autoimmune diseases are just a few of its health-related consequences. Bottling emotion is like trying to stop the wind — no matter what, it's going to blow. You don't always know when or where.

Feelings Are Basic

Feelings are basic and instinctive, and just like any other mammal, humans experience feelings first on a physiological level and then very often have automatic responses to the feelings. A dog wags its tail when happy or hopeful; a cat hisses when chased by a dog; a horse rears up when crossing paths with a snake; a human yells when angry. This type of animal instinct serves to protect you; mammals with large brains can be trained or conditioned to respond in particular ways. You can train a horse not to throw its rider when it hears an unexpected noise; you can also train a child to suppress his anger because you believe it's "socially unacceptable." You're capable of having several feelings at once. You can train yourself to ignore one of those simultaneous feelings at your own expense to satisfy a desire. Watch any *Lifetime* movie for a dramatic reenactment of the consequences of ignoring "fear" when feeling "love."

A frightened horse doesn't judge itself by thinking, "I'm such a baby. I really shouldn't get so upset about snakes," but he can be trained to react in a less anxious manner. You, too, should not judge yourself for your feelings and it's comforting to know that you, too, can train yourself to react to people and situations in a less emotional, more rational way.

Feelings serve a purpose just as your vital organs do. They provide a sense of meaning and relevance to the world around you. I believe feelings are a gift, not a curse or something you should diligently try to avoid. Inherently, they're neither good nor bad; they give you information so you know how to interact with the world around you. For example:

- LOVE gives you a sense of CONNECTION to your partner, babies, nature, art, etc.
- FEAR gives you PROTECTION, a warning that danger is imminent.

- ANGER gives you STRENGTH and prompts you to ACTION.
- PAIN provides an opportunity for HEALING and GROWTH.
- SHAME helps you realize I'M NO BETTER OR WORSE than anyone else.
- GUILT calls you back to our CORE VALUES.
- JOY provides RESTORATION and HEALING.
- LONELINESS prompts you to REACH OUT, be VULNERABLE and CONNECT to others.

You learned in Chapter Three that one of the first goals of therapy is to establish and enlarge your basic self. The first step in doing this is acknowledging your feelings and labeling them in a non-judgmental way. Instead of feeling so angry that you punch a wall, or feeling shame so you drink, or feeling lonely so you withdraw, it becomes, "I feel angry. This is me, feeling angry. This is anger. It's just a feeling. This, too, shall pass. In what way do I want to use the strength that this anger is providing me?" Engaging your intellect about your feelings allows you to manage them more efficiently. You gain power over them versus the other way around.

There is debate over whether emotions precede thoughts (*EMOTION ➔ THOUGHTS ➔BEHAVIOR*) or thoughts come first (*THOUGHT ➔ EMOTION ➔BEHAVIOR).* What is important is that we know the difference between the two and understand how to use our thoughts to help process and manage our emotions.

Some research suggests there are six primary emotions: love, joy, fear, anger, pain and surprise (each with associated other feelings) but there are several schools of thought on this subject. Here's a list of some of the primary feelings (underlined) and underneath, their closely related counterparts:

<u>Love</u>	<u>Joy</u>	<u>Fear</u>
Lust	Pride	Nervousness
Compassion	Hope	Anxiety

Anger	Pain	Surprise
Rage	Sadness	Awe
Frustration	Regret	Astonishment

Dr. Terry Hargrave's theory of Restoration Therapy maintains that the two primal feelings of love and safety (sometimes called trustworthiness) are not only the cornerstone of all healthy relationships, but also primary needs to human existence.[11] Let's look at this therapeutic approach for a moment.

A child who feels loved by his family will probably also feel valued and unique. When he experiences safety, he knows that he can count on his family and will strive to do the same for them. He doesn't need to spend his time pursuing potentially harmful means in order to feel loved or establish safety. He knows that he has others he can depend on and whether he gets an "A" at school or a "C" will not diminish their feelings for him. He's confident that if his parents tell him they'll pick him up at five o'clock, they will. He also knows that if the family rule is such that there is no name calling, then there isn't. In other words, he trusts that what his family says and does match up. When love and safety are present in your original caregivers, your basic identity is profoundly influenced and shaped into a healthier individual.

But when either love or safety is lacking from original caregivers, a person's basic identity is profoundly influenced and shaped into a less healthy individual. Individuals are "left to cope with the loss of love through identity struggles" and "with the loss of trustworthiness through dependence on self."[12] Whether you experience a violation of love or one of safety, what happens is you then end up having difficult feelings triggered over and over again in your lifetime by current relationships or situations. Because of fight or flight responses to basic needs not being met, you act out with coping behaviors that range from blaming others to shaming yourself, or from controlling behaviors to chaotic behaviors.

Let's say a young person experiences a tremendous loss of predictability in his family; for example, his mother left the family when he was in grade school. The lack of the primary need of safety being met by his primary caretaker in turn requires him to find a way to feel safe. Unfortunately, the behaviors that he learns as a coping strategy may be unhealthy, such as perhaps becoming perfectionistic, performance driven and judgmental. So when he experiences something as small as a grocery store clerk ignoring him, he experiences the feeling of rejection, which triggers a feeling of the lack of safety and he in turn behaves by speaking in an angry and aggressive manner to the store clerk.

The goal, then, of restoration therapy is to identify previous sources of pain caused by feeling unloved or unsafe, confront old messages (e.g., "I am in danger in this situation") with new messages from an adult perspective (e.g., "I am safe in this situation"), and so choose healthier behaviors. This is also called "self-" or "re-parenting." Though you can't go back and change the past, you can challenge and change existing patterns and behavior within yourself.

Mismanaging Feelings

Paying attention to your feelings is vital for your emotional health. When a person is more focused on his feelings than on his thoughts, he runs the risk of being governed or overrun by those feelings. For most of us, this creates suffering. Further, he is more likely to abandon his own principles in an attempt to please others. More suffering ensues.

However, when he learns to use his intellect to help him manage his feelings — that is to say, when he applies the thinking process to what he's feeling — he becomes more fully aware of his feelings and yet he's able to process them in an open, honest and non-judgmental way. He has more choices about how then to behave. By doing so, feelings become just feelings, experiences which are allowed to be felt, and then released — rather than trying to ignore them or wrestle with an impulse for immediate and anxiety-infused action. Failure to manage feelings inevitably shows up not only in yourself but also in your relationships.

Jeffrey is a successful realtor, married to Beverly, with two young children. They're a loving family but Jeffrey has a hot temper. He jokes about it, admitting he frequently loses his cool in even minor situations but minimizes it by saying, "At least I don't hold grudges." To calm himself after a typical explosion, he grabs a beer (or three) and heads to his garage workshop.

His wife and kids walk on eggshells around Jeffrey. They'd rather hide certain truths from him than risk the brunt of his wrath. Beverly in particular feels a heavy obligation to keep the peace within the household. Because Jeffrey does not think his anger is a problem, his family is left to deal with the consequences.

Louise has been with her partner Will for ten years. Will is a generally pleasant person with one very annoying habit, at least as far as Louise is concerned: Every time they get together with friends, he says something embarrassing about her. It might not be anything "big" at least as far as he's concerned — last week, he told everyone what a klutz she is at sports; a few months ago, he had the group in stitches with stories of her mother's terrible cooking and how Louise must have inherited her "skills." Louise smiles and goes along with it but inside, she feels mortified. She has mentioned her feelings to Will a few times but he ignores her. Lately, when social invitations come their way, Louise feigns a headache or says she's too busy with work to join in, so Will goes without her.

Through these examples and perhaps your own, I hope you can see the importance of acknowledging, managing and sharing your feelings with those with whom you're in relationship. When we do not take these essential steps toward self-care, we do not honor our most basic needs.

Summing Up

When you understand that feelings are automatic and provide us with needed information, you can learn to embrace and apply your thinking skills to them rather than avoid feelings or let them run your life. This is an important part of the therapeutic process.

Workout

Grab your journal and find a quiet spot. Close your eyes and relax, breathing in and out slowly for a minute or two. Think of a time when you felt "love" — unconditional, all-encompassing love. Now visualize "love". What does it look like to you? Is it a traditional symbol like a red, beating heart or something more abstract? Scan your body and notice where you have physical sensations of love. Where are they and what do they feel like? Write down in your journal how and where you felt "love." What do you feel in your body? Does your head feel light? Is your heart beating fast? Where in your body do you feel the feeling and how?

Additional Reps

Repeat this exercise with "anger", "guilt", "pride" and "surprise."

CHAPTER 5

DIFFERENTIATION OF SELF

Come Here — Now, Go Away!

We don't see things as they are. We see things as we are.
— Anaïs Nin

Make sure you visualize what you really want,
not what someone else wants for you.
— Jerry Gillies

In Chapter Three, I referenced Dr. Murray Bowen's family systems theory, which considers the tension between the desire to be autonomous and the simultaneous desire to be attached to others. According to Dr. Bowen, a person is "differentiated" to the extent that he can separate his own cognitive processing (thinking) and emotional processing (feeling) from that of his family.[13] The extent to which he will be able to do this is equal to his ability to differentiate between his own thinking and his own feeling. Furthering Dr. Bowen's theory, relationship expert Rokelle Lerner describes the "practical issues of maintaining our separateness and the sacred domain of connection… not [as] a duality, but a continuum of the whole."[14] Though being in meaningful relationships is the icing on life's cake, if you will, you must first learn how to balance the desire to be autonomous and the desire to be attached, if your relationships are to be a source of pleasure and not pain.

Stress and anxiety often arise from our inability to maintain balance between these desires (autonomy and attachment) and from failure to establish healthy boundaries. Over- or under-attaching to others can create just as many problems as over- or under-autonomy. You wrestle balancing with the need to feel important and loved with the need *not* to feel smothered or confined, just as you struggle with pursuing your own pleasures while not ignoring your loved ones.

Often when life troubles develop, you instinctively know you must do something different from what you've always done before. That something is changing your level of differentiation (which I'll explain a bit later in this chapter), which, by the way, is by no means an easy task. But I believe it's absolutely possible when you're motivated and willing to do the necessary work.

The level of differentiation that you have achieved when you leave home, typically as a young adult, is the level at which you will tend to remain throughout your life. That is, except to the extent that you learn how to manage the tension between your need for autonomy and your need for attachment. This knowledge may come from introspection, reflection, support groups, or any other process conducive to "growing yourself up." Therapy is one such process.

Interestingly, the people with whom you willingly choose to spend your time — whether intimate, personal or professional in nature — tend to be, more or less, at your same level of differentiation or emotional maturity. You may find comfort in knowing, however, that when it comes to increasing your differentiation, you need only to focus on your own progress; no one else's.

Now, look at Figure 5, the Scale of Differentiation[15]. The Scale of Differentiation shows the relationship between the two primary forces we've been talking about: the need to be an individual (autonomy), and the need to go along with others and be part of a relationship or group (attachment), and the difference between emotional processing and cognitive (thinking) processing.

At a lower level of differentiation, a person will feel more internal pressure to abandon his own autonomy and vital needs in order to conform to others, while at a higher level he is better able to remain autonomous while engaging as a functioning member of the group in a close and intimate way. How well we manage the tension between the opposing needs for autonomy and attachment reflects how well-differentiated we are. With increased self-differentiation, it becomes easier to maintain that tension in a healthy, loving way.

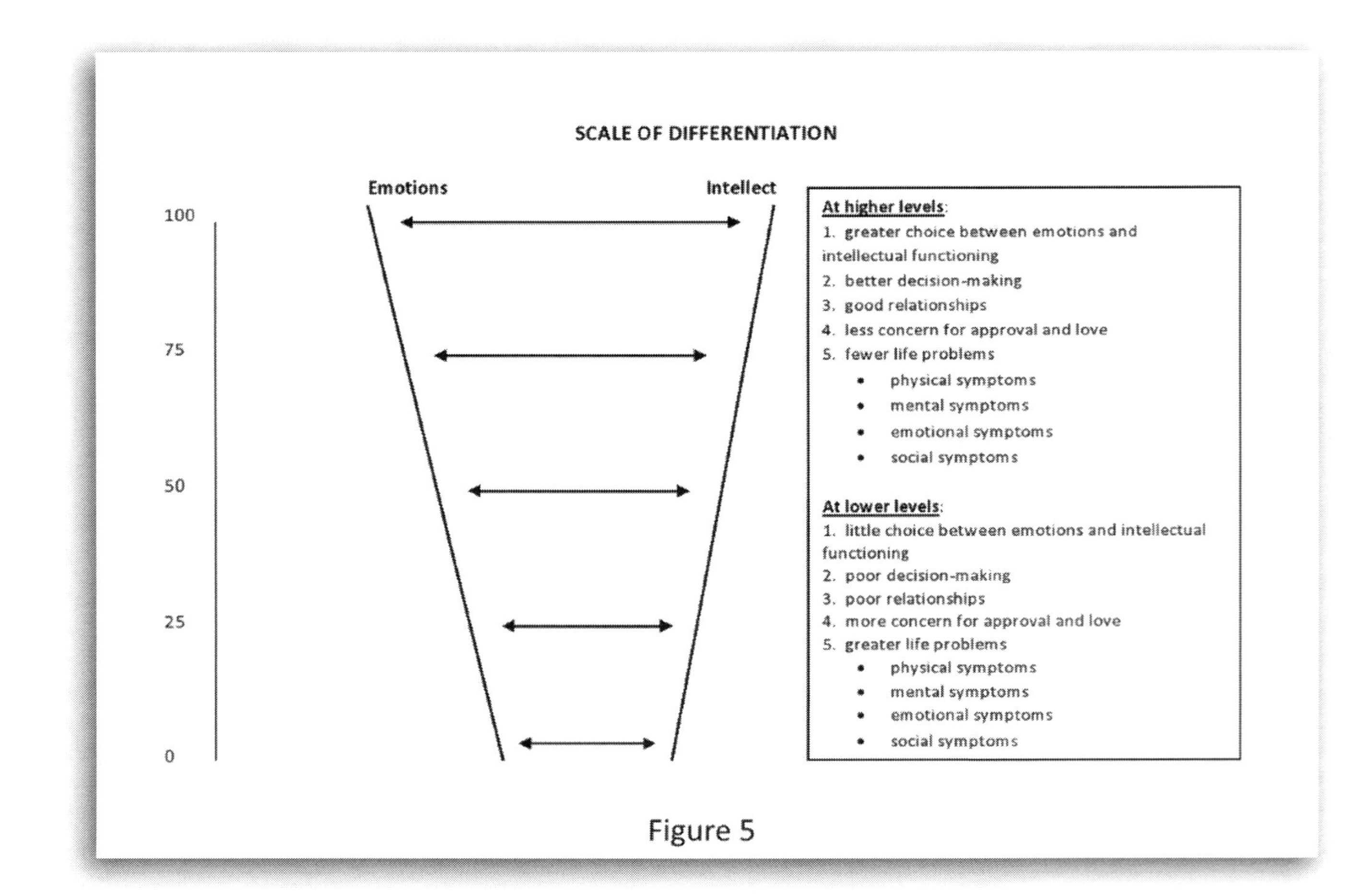
SCALE OF DIFFERENTIATION
Emotions
Intellect
100
75
50
25
0
At higher levels:
1. greater choice between emotions and intellectual functioning
2. better decision-making
3. good relationships
4. less concern for approval and love
5. fewer life problems
• physical symptoms
• mental symptoms
• emotional symptoms
• social symptoms
At lower levels:
1. little choice between emotions and intellectual functioning
2. poor decision-making
3. poor relationships
4. more concern for approval and love
5. greater life problems
• physical symptoms
• mental symptoms
• emotional symptoms
• social symptoms

Figure 5

Poorly Differentiated

People who are poorly differentiated are often the folks who say, "Me? I'd *never* go to therapy!" That's not to say that they wouldn't benefit from it. Some of them typically navigate through their lives as if they are like a flapper on a pinball machine — unthinkingly or emotionally flapping out at life's challenges — rather than planning for, or really dealing with, life's challenges. They fail to balance between their emotions with their intellect. They tend to base their decisions on emotion, have poor decision-making skills, and are highly concerned about approval, acceptance and love. On a side note, intelligence has very little to do with where a person falls on the Scale of Differentiation.

Their relationships tend to fall into one of two categories: either they're highly enmeshed/co-dependent, or they're completely cut off (all or nothing behavior). Co-dependent relationships have difficulty functioning in a healthy way and often leave both parties feeling frustrated. Relationships that are terminated abruptly by one or both parties, rather than dealing with problems as they arise, unfortunately tend to stay very much alive in us emotionally; the relationship is simply replaced with resentment.

When undifferentiated, people tend to suffer greater life problems and spend their time blaming others — often portraying themselves as victims. It's not uncommon for them to ignore or diminish their feelings toward others' actions and words.

Well Differentiated

At this level, the basic self is well developed. A well differentiated person doesn't struggle with self-confidence issues and his relationships are healthy because he knows how to establish boundaries and not take things too personally, while at the same time he is vulnerable, intimate and authentic. He's free to move through life with compassion, yet he's unburdened by the opinions and demands of others.

Most therapy clients fall somewhere in the middle on the scale. Let's take a look at Lisa.

Living in the Middle

Lisa began therapy with a somewhat underdeveloped basic self. As a child, her father always spoke for her, ordered her meals and told her when she was being "too sensitive" or "not competitive enough." As a now thirty-year old woman, her father still calls most of the shots in her life. He's still the first person she consults when offered a new position at work or when she wants to paint her apartment and is unsure of the color or type of paint. He doesn't offer suggestions but rather tells her what to do and even though she frequently complains to me about it, she allows it because she worries that if she defies his wishes, she will be unlovable to him.

Lisa vacillates frequently between relying heavily on her father's opinion and questioning whether she should get him out of her life altogether because he has so much power over her. His every comment or action concerning her affects Lisa in an extremely negative way. She has suffered from migraines for years and admitted that in college, she'd struggled with anorexia. In fact, it's not unusual for a person who feels out of control in one area of her life (in Lisa's case, her relationship with her father) to turn around and behave in a very controlling manner elsewhere (e.g., by restricting her food intake and over-exercising) in an attempt to manage other people's roles and situations in our lives.

Over time, Lisa and I began to shift the focus of our sessions from "What my dad said or did" to "What I *thought and felt* about what he said or did." It was a small shift in our actual conversations but a significant shift for her. Because her father had always made most of her decisions for her, she hadn't spent much time pondering what she actually thought or why. We also addressed the fact that even though she was now a grown woman, she still sought out her father's opinion, which inevitably turned into a mandate. She'd convinced herself that if she bypassed this step and made a decision by herself, she would undoubtedly make the wrong choice and disappoint and infuriate her father for not asking him in the first place. Then, he would have to swoop in correct the problem — like the time she searched for her first apartment after college and put a deposit on one in a neighborhood that her dad didn't like. He took a landlord to small claims court to get her money back and apparently, this incident taught her a "valuable" lesson: Don't do anything for yourself or you'll screw it up and someone will have to rescue you.

Lisa loved her father but was ready to make a change in the way she related to him. We talked about the boundaries of their relationship and how she might go about reconstructing them. We also talked about risk: of losing his approval, of trying things (and making mistakes) on her own, of not always being able to remedy mistakes but the value of making them, and of taking charge of her own life including her relationships, job and financial responsibilities — without using dad as a perpetual safety net. To move forward with her life and her relationship with her parent, Lisa had to learn to take and get comfortable with these things. She had become more differentiated.

Summing Up

A person who is well-differentiated recognizes the difference between his thoughts and feelings and those of others. He's able to let others have their own experiences while he has. He's better able to navigate around life's conflicts both inside and outside his relationships, staying true to himself and not succumbing to the demands or preferences of others.

Workout

Go back to Chapter Two and look at the family genogram you drew. Consider each relationship in your genogram in terms of the Scale of Differentiation we discuss in this chapter. How do your family members tend to behave? Are they highly autonomous? Highly attached? Or, they fall somewhere in the middle? Recognizing the patterns of attachment in your own family system is an important step in understanding your ability (or struggle) to maintain balance between the opposing desires.

CHAPTER 6

MANAGING FEELINGS

"Neither Good Nor Bad"

What we achieve inwardly will change our outer reality.
— *Plutarch*

When you begin to understand that much of your unhappiness, both in and out of relationships, stems from an imbalance of conflicting desires to be alone and *not* be alone, you can also begin to address the symptoms of the imbalance. You're still working toward your ultimate goal, which is to enlarge your basic self so that you're less reactive to the emotional whims and demands of other people. You're learning to engage your thought process when processing emotions so that they do not rule you. Now, you're ready to explore healthier ways to manage your feelings.

Where to Begin?

For people who've spent many years sweeping their feelings under the rug, learning to manage feelings can seem a task of epic proportion. I remember a young man named Carl who was told his entire childhood that "anger" is what "bad" people feel, so he never allowed himself to feel it and felt shame if he did. As an adult, he had a very difficult time acknowledging when he was indeed mad as hell at someone, and then expressing his anger in a healthy way. He struggled with one extreme or the other: Either he used sarcasm to deflect his true feelings, or bent clubs in two when he missed a shot during a friendly game of golf. Both extremes left Carl's friends and girlfriend wondering what he was so upset about. The smallest things seemed to set him off and they'd begun withdrawing from him, leaving him feeling isolated.

In therapy, Carl learned that feelings are neither good nor bad, they're just feelings. Feelings may be pleasant or unpleasant, but they are an innate part of every person. Likewise people who have feelings are neither "good" nor "bad." A goal of therapy is to recognize your feelings as they begin to arise and then to manage them appropriately. Taking away the stigma he'd learned in childhood about feelings, particularly anger, was very freeing to Carl. When it becomes okay to express feelings, Carl learned to use his energy to process them and let them go, rather than trying to fight them.

Giving yourself permission to experience and express feelings is one of the best things you can do for yourself. Here are some suggestions for getting started with managing feelings:

Learn How to Breathe

Managing feelings begins with the breath. Imagine any movie or television scene where a crisis is being played out. What is the first thing the hero or medical technician almost always tells the person in crisis? *Breathe! Just breathe!* Yes, there are numerous other ways to alleviate stress such as taking a warm bath, listening to classical music and getting a soothing massage, but when you're out on a limb, the only available tool you may have in that moment is your breath. Use it! Studies have shown that deep, purposeful, intentional breathing is not only highly relaxing, it affects in a positive way every organ and function in your body and may even affect gene expression.

Workout

There's a breathing exercise that many people find helpful called 1-4-2, meaning the length of time for breath holding is 4 times the inhalation time, and the length of exhale is twice as long as the inhalation time. For you, it might look like this:

Breathe in for two seconds
Hold breath for eight seconds
Release breath for four seconds

Practicing this technique several times a day is a powerful tool, particularly in managing anxiety.

Practice Awareness

As soon as you notice an uncomfortable emotion, notice the accompanying physiological (felt) sensations in your body. Is your gut in knots (fear)? Does your chest feel heavy (sadness) or tight (anger)? Is your heart beating faster? Is you breathing deeper or shallower? Do you feel an adrenaline rush? How does your body feel when you experience more pleasant emotions? Are there happy butterflies dancing in your tummy (love)? These sensations are built-in signals that our feelings are present and need our attention. Examine the felt sensations accompanying emotions, and do this intentionally and mindfully.

Choose Feeling Words Intentionally

Any time you say or think the words, "I feel…", be sure the next word after "feel" is an emotion, not an action. For example, you might say, "I feel fearful (or anxious) that I am not going to finish my assignment on time," rather than, "I feel really rushed with my assignment." The word "feel" serves as a cue that you're about to express an emotion.

Don't Fight It

Remind yourself that feelings come and go like the wind; they will pass. When you try to fight uncomfortable feelings, particularly the sensations of anxiety or panic, you give them more energy. They quickly become the pink elephant in the room you're trying so desperately *not* to think about. When you just ignore them, they will show up in other, not necessarily healthy, ways. Just because you feel something unpleasant doesn't mean you necessarily have to do anything about it. Just notice it. Let it come, let it be, and let it go.

Remain Neutral

If you apply judgment, especially in a negative way, to a feeling ("I feel I'm bad that I dislike my in-laws"), you often set about trying to obliterate it without actually processing it.

Try not to judge your feelings. Even when you feel something that is uncomfortable, remind yourself that emotions are not "right" or "wrong" — they just "are." Sit with it and notice how the emotion feels in your body. Remember, you can choose to act — or not — on any feeling, and the timing is up to you.

Become a Trained Observer

Once you've become more aware of your feelings, say to yourself, "This is me, feeling ______________ (whatever emotion is experienced)" or even simply "This is ________________ (whatever emotion is experienced)." If you're accustomed to judging your feelings and/or dismissing them, this will be quite a departure for you. By practicing this step regularly, you'll eventually learn to "go" with your feelings rather than constantly trying to fight or change them.

Incorporate Healthy Self-Soothing Techniques

Take for example a baby who is crying with gusto in his crib. His parent may feel the need to rush in, pick up the baby, cuddle him and help him stop crying. This of course is not bad parenting — in fact, it's very loving parenting. But it doesn't allow the baby to help *himself* stop crying. What if instead, the parent checked on the baby, smiled at him, patted him on the tummy, turned on some soothing music and left the room? In this scenario, the baby is more likely to look for his thumb to suck, or a pacifier, or maybe a blanket to cuddle. In other words, he is learning to depend on himself to feel better. This is a form of "self-soothing."

The same can be said for adults. If you're always looking for a purchase, a substance or even another person to make you feel happier/more loved/validated, etc., you miss a wonderful opportunity to provide these things for yourself and end up causing yourself further pain.

Healthy self-soothing techniques include deep breathing, meditation or prayer, listening to calming music, taking a warm bath and even just unplugging for an hour or two.

Journaling

Journaling is a great way to observe emotions and process through them. When you release emotions, they lose power. See the next chapter on journaling to get you started.

Summing Up

Feelings are neither good nor bad but they are very important. Learning to accept feelings as they come and go, without judgment, is critical in learning to manage them so that you're in charge of them — and not the other way around.

CHAPTER 7

THE IMPORTANCE OF JOURNALING

Seeing is Believing

To find out what is truly individual in ourselves, profound reflection is needed; and suddenly we realize how uncommonly difficult the discovery of individuality in fact is.
— CARL JUNG

Ahhh, journaling. To my creative, right-brained clients who enjoy writing, journaling is something to which they can actually learn to look forward. It's not a source of torture to them; it comes quite naturally. But to my clients who would rather speak nude in front of thousands of people than sit down on a regular basis with pen and paper describing their feelings, journaling can seem an arduous and pointless task. However I, among many other therapists, believe that journaling is a very important tool that can be used to enhance the therapeutic process and I strongly encourage you to give it a try.

Journaling initiates the process of introspection, the examination or observation of your own thoughts and feelings. The act of writing actually engages the intellectual part of the brain. Events happen to each one of us. You then develop thoughts and feelings about these events that you may not even realize and that have the capability of either being psychologically healthy or unhealthy for you. Journaling allows you to examine what language you use to tell your story: Do you use victim words to describe your past? Do you see patterns where you're overly controlling? Are you especially concerned about others' feelings and opinions?

Why Journaling is So Important

Rewriting your authentic life story as it happens is not about erasing the past but about understanding how past events and relationships have shaped the person you are today, then reframing and reprioritizing the meaning of those events so that they serve you in a positive rather than negative way. Journaling gives you the chance to review and retell your story, to actually see it in writing — forcing you to get more specific about thoughts and feelings that may have been vague. It promotes both ownership and a renewed sense of awareness about where you're coming from.

But awareness is only the first stage of change. Limiting and destructive behavioral patterns are like bad habits, difficult to break without concentrated effort. For example, you *know* that exercise and eating nutritious foods are healthy things for your body. You can sit down with a notebook and write extensively about how much you want to lose weight and list *ad nauseum* all the failed diets of your past. You can devise an eating plan that would make Dr. Oz proud and map out an exercise regime that will have you, theoretically, in tip-top shape. But if you're an emotional eater who raids the pantry every time you feel sad or depressed or anxious, you're going to have a difficult time staying out of the cookie jar and putting your plan into action. Unfortunately, until you come to terms with your story, you're more than likely to repeat it, just like our friend in *Groundhog Day*.

In Chapter Three I talked briefly about the stages of change, which are:

- Precontemplation – not even thinking there is a problem or need for change.
- Contemplation – willingness to consider the possibility of a problem or need for change.

- Determination – Making a commitment to action; being ready to change.
- Action – Putting a plan into action.
- Maintenance – Firmly establishing the new plan; dealing with relapses toward old behavior.
- Termination – Old behavior or problem ceases.

Journaling is one of the ways that you may express an idea regarding change, or you may actually use it to contemplate it. Your journal can help you move from contemplation to determination, lay out a plan of action and support your goals.

But it's not only the *telling* of your story (whether verbally or by journal writing) that is an integral part of your progress. It's also taking ownership of your story and perhaps becoming more *aware* that it's no longer working to your benefit. Finally, you get better by using the tools learned in therapy to write a different story for the future.

Challenging Core Beliefs Through Journaling

Though I'm guessing your story has many details involving ups and downs, it may also have one or two (or more) over-riding themes or core beliefs that go with it. Some examples may include:

- Things always fall apart for me.
- Nothing ever works in my favor.
- It was bound to go bad eventually.
- I'll be happy when…
- People always take advantage of me.
- I'll never have a healthy, loving relationship.
- I can't depend on anyone.
- My loved ones will abandon me if I don't agree with them.
- I'll never have enough

Consciously or unconsciously, these themes shape your experience of the world. You carry around these heavy, burdensome themes, which manage to work their way into your life on a regular basis. Many times, because these themes are so ingrained in you, you don't even stop to consider what price they're extracting from your life. Journaling helps you recognize these themes or core beliefs.

Journaling allows you to go back and review your thoughts and feelings and find negative behavioral patterns and cracks in your thinking. When you uncover the theme that is following you relentlessly, you can go to work adjusting its message and the way it makes you feel. Let's do that for the themes listed above:

- Replace *Things always fall apart for me* with…
  I've had challenges but I'm a stronger person because of them.
- Replace *Nothing ever works in my favor* with…
  I am the author of my own life and deserve good things.
- Replace *It was bound to go bad eventually* with…
  I cannot predict the future; I can only make a decision to live more fully today.
- Replace *I'll be happy when…*with…
  I am happy with myself just as I am today.
- Replace *People always take advantage of me* with…
  I am learning how to set healthy boundaries and establish mutually respectful relationships.
- Replace *I'll never have a healthy, loving relationship* with…
  I deserve love and am lovable.
- Replace *I can't depend on anyone* with…
  It's okay to ask for what I want, even if I don't always get it. I am resourceful.
- Replace *My loved ones will abandon me if I don't agree with them* with…
  It's okay to have a different opinion from my loved ones. I am lovable just as I am.
- Replace *I'll never have enough* with…
  I always have enough and I know how to take good care of myself.

Do you see how these small changes in the statements you make about yourself might lead to bigger changes in the way you perceive your story and even the world around you? Can you imagine that replacing previously held core beliefs with a more loving and accepting version might even alter the way you retell your story in the future? When you take the time to challenge your core beliefs, you sometimes find they were never really yours in the first place.

In the telling of your story, it's quite common to think in black and white terms. Let's say you've been going through life believing "Nothing ever works out for me." Then I ask you to talk and journal about this belief. You make a list of your perceived failures and next to it, your successes. You may be surprised to see that the "success" list is actually noticeably longer than the "failure" list.

It's not so much the actual events of your life that become your story. You use inner dialogue to repeat and expand hurts and failures, over and over, until you have branded yourself and can't escape, becoming one and the same with a particular event. It's kind of like an actor who plays a memorable role in a movie, then no matter how many great movies he makes before or after that role, it is the one for which he will always be known. It's also possible to typecast yourself.

Past events are just that. You can't go back in time and change what has happened to you. But you can change the way you think and feel about those events. That's what journaling in therapy allows you to do.

Workout

In your journal, write down three to five of your own core beliefs that might come to mind when reading this chapter. In a second column, write a statement to counter each belief. Next to each, add one or two sentences about where (or from whom) the belief may have originated. Was it yours all along, or did you borrow it from someone else?

Resistance to Change

If you know your story is no longer working for you, it seems logical that you'd want to make changes. But if it were that easy, you would have done it a long time ago, saving yourself a great deal of grief and frustration. Therapy can help. So can journaling.

We're all human and can be terribly resistant to change, even when it promises to bring improvement to our lives. Add to that distorted thinking and it can be very difficult, indeed. You may have become quite adept at coming up with all kinds of "reasons" why making changes might be possible for other people, but certainly not for yourself:

- I don't want to pretend to be I'm someone I'm not. I'm just not a glass-half-full type of person.
- Maybe I'd be able to see my story differently if so many bad things hadn't actually happened to me!
- My story isn't my fault — I was a victim of circumstance.
- How do I possibly put a positive spin on abandonment/lifelong panic attacks/being raised by alcoholics/illness/loved one's death/financial devastation, etc.?

Most of us build our stories in small increments — to protect ourselves from further emotional pain, as a way to try to make sense of things that we don't understand. Our beliefs are what we tell ourselves repeatedly until we're convinced that they're true. You didn't create your own beliefs out of thin air because you're a terrible, dishonest or pretentious person, or because you enjoy others' pity. They served a purpose at one time but their usefulness eventually expires.

The story in the previous chapter that Lisa wrote about herself was that she was a basically helpless adult who couldn't fight her own battles or make sound decisions. It began innocently enough — as a little girl's way to win her father's affection. Through a series of seemingly harmless events, she inadvertently set herself up for a relationship that robbed her of her independence. Lisa also came to believe that important relationships must be based on "if/

then" conditions: "If I listen to dad's advice, then I won't fail," and "If I don't fail, then he will love me."

Lisa's story was reinforced when she attempted to strike out on her own by finding an apartment, only to have her dad veto her choice, then take charge of getting her money back for her. When you rely too heavily on other people and their opinions to determine your self-worth, it's all too easy to blame a mistake on your stupidity, incompetence, or worthlessness rather than seeing it for what it really is: a mistake; we all make them. In healthy family systems, we're even *encouraged* to do so in order to learn from them. Lisa was not allowed to make mistakes even as a child. Daddy was right there to protect her from all hurt. Now, Lisa is dealing with the consequences of his overprotection.

Through journaling, Lisa began to see that many of her core beliefs were simply not true. She was able to come up with positive statements about herself as the woman she is today that are much more accurate. I want to point out here that there is a difference between core beliefs and core values — they sometimes are used interchangeably but they're not the same thing.

A *belief* is something that you've told yourself over and over and accept it as truth. A *value* is something that you hold as extremely important to your authenticity. When you violate a core value, you feel shame, guilt and a sense that you're not being true to who you really are. But changing a long-held belief that no longer serves you actually moves you toward a more authentic self.

Additional Reps

In your journal, write down your top five core *values*. Compare your values to your core *beliefs* and see how they might be different. Do your values influence your beliefs or vice versa? Can you use your values to make your beliefs feel more authentic? Here are some examples of core values:

Adventure	Autonomy
Challenge	Change
Community	Competence
Competition	Cooperation
Creativity	Decisiveness
Diversity	Ecology/Environment
Education	Ethics
Excellence	Excitement
Fairness	Fame
Family	Flexibility
Freedom	Friendship.
Happiness	Health
Helping Others	Honesty
Independence	Integrity
Leadership	Loyalty
Meaningful Work	Money
Order	Philanthropy
Play	Pleasure
Power	Privacy
Recognition	Relationships
Religion	Safety
Security	Service
Spirituality	Stability
Status	Wealth
Work	

Types of Journals

Among my clients, the number one reason they struggle with journaling is that they simply "don't know where to begin." It's a valid concern, I think, especially for clients who are not accustomed to writing in general or to thinking in detail about their feelings. Your journal should reflect your personality and what feels most comfortable to you in the expression of your thoughts and feelings. There are many ways to journal. Here are some ideas to get started:

Fill in the Blanks Journal

This is a good option for people who either don't enjoy writing or believe they don't have time to journal on a regular basis. Simply create a one page "fill in the blanks" with prompts that will get you in touch with your feelings for the day, and place it in a binder. Make copies, one for each day of the month. Some examples are:

How I feel about myself today is ________________________.
Have I honored myself and others today and, if so, how?
Did I ask for what I wanted today and if not, why?
Today's challenges included ________________________.
Today's victories included ________________________.
What I learned about myself or someone else today:
What I am thankful for is ________________________.

Feelings Journal

When clients are having a difficult time getting started with journaling, I always say start with the most basic, yet important, element — your feelings. I'm not talking about Shakespearean examples of grandiose sentiment; I'm referring to a simple journal that includes listing your feelings; for example, something that describes how you felt when your takeout order was completely messed up and you didn't say anything. Or, when your mother told you that she wished you would change your hair color. Start with recent events (big or small). If you can't think of anything to say about these events, simply record them in chronological order — at least you'll get in the habit of writing in your journal on a daily basis. Try to leave out any speculation on *why* someone did something, or whether he did it on purpose, or how he may have felt about it — focus only on how *you* felt at the time.

Examples of Feelings Journal entries:

> *Thursday, June 20*
> *Best friend told me she was having dinner party with her book club friends. It's not that I don't want her to have fun but I feel left out and a little angry that I am not invited.*
>
> *Friday, June 21*
>
> *Received praise at work today for the project I've been working on for three months. I feel a little embarrassed by the attention but also proud of my efforts.*

A *feelings journal* is a simple yet powerful tool to begin the process of recognizing what fuels our thoughts, opinions and actions toward yourself and others. Another way of doing this is by filling in these blanks:

1. This happened: ______________________________.
2. I felt ___________ and I then did ______________.

   Or,

1. This happened: ______________________________.
2. I thought ___________________________________.
3. I felt _______________________________________.
4. I did _______________________________________.

Thoughts Journal

A *thoughts journal* (also called a Cognitive Behavioral Thoughts Journal) is a type of journal that takes a feelings journal a step further by analyzing how or why you feel a certain way. The idea behind both the feelings and thoughts journal is to assist you in learning the vital skill of how to differentiate between thoughts and feelings, something I talk about in detail in Chapter Four. Thoughts journals can be helpful in a variety of ways but especially so in recognizing and processing through repetitive negative behavioral patterns such as an eating disorder, alcohol or drug addiction, or compulsive shopping.

Examples of a Thoughts Journal entry:

> *Saturday, June 22*
> *Read a style magazine this morning and it made me want to buy new clothes, even though I know I don't need them. I thought about how some of the new trends would work well with my figure. I drove to the mall and let myself window shop for an hour. I felt anxious and guilty because I knew I was going to buy something I couldn't afford. I spent over $1,000.00 in thirty minutes. I felt extremely guilty but also almost "high." Of course, I plan to return half of the things that I bought. Even though I initially love the excitement that buying things brings me, the guilt that I feel afterwards is crushing. I'm not going to kick myself over this, but instead admit that looking at fashion magazines and hanging out at malls might not be helpful to my progress.*

Notice how, in this entry, feelings are considered before, during and after an event and rationale is applied without judgment. This is an important step for the person who either hides certain feelings because he judges them as "bad" or unacceptable, or for someone who acts impulsively based on feelings.

Letter Journal

Some of my clients prefer to journal in the style of a letter to me, such as "Dear Mary…". With your therapist in mind as the recipient of your letter, you can sort of continue your last session with your therapist and stay in touch with him until the time of the next session.

Letter journals can also be written to the people in your life with whom you're struggling in a relationship, and to those who are no longer in your life yet continue to cause you suffering. It's not necessary to read or show these letters to the person to whom they're addressed.

Narrative Journal

If you enjoy writing stories or poetry, try a narrative journal. You tell your own story as though you're writing someone else's biography. You can be either the main character, a secondary character or even the narrator.

Poetry Journal

Express your thoughts and feelings through poetry, sonnets, or quotes about yourself, nature, other people, etc. Even if you've never written this type of thing before, you may be surprised how much you enjoy it and how meaningful it becomes.

Non-Written Journals

If you're not a word person, no worries. There are many other types of journals that you're free to explore, including:

Art Journal

Drawing, doodling, painting, beading, sewing, photography and mixed media are just a few of the artistic ways to express yourself. Google "art journals" and be inspired by others' creativity.

Meditative Art Journal

Similar to art journals but before each entry, you practice getting into a meditative state — then allow your brain to create whatever it wants to create in that moment. It's a spiritual practice in the process of creating.

Sharing Your Journal with Your Therapist

Yet another reason that regular journaling is so important is that it helps hold you accountable to yourself. You're creating a written basis for honest communication, proof that you're becoming more aware of, and taking responsibility for, your experiences. It works in the same way that, for example, a food diary does for someone who is trying to lose weight. By being honest about every bite of food eaten throughout the day (even when it's "cheating"), the dieter is better able to identify triggers to overeating. When you're honest about your thoughts and behavior in your journal, you'll learn to recognize negative patterns that are keeping you from your goals. Ultimately, though, your journal is more for you than it is for your therapist. It keeps the process of change going and growing between sessions.

Resist the urge to edit your journal, even if you've written something about which you're ashamed or with which your therapist might not agree. You're not writing your journal to gain your therapist's approval; you're doing so to feel and get better.

Summing Up

With practice and commitment, you *can* learn to change negative thought patterns, tolerate unpleasant feelings and gain a better understanding of your life both as it's and as you wish it to be; journaling is a helpful exercise toward these worthy endeavors.

CHAPTER 8

RELATIONSHIP PATTERNS

Healthy Relationships Require Healthy People

Before healing others, heal yourself.
-LAO TZU

As a marriage and family therapist, I see relationship difficulties every day. More often than not, those difficulties involve idealized notions of what relationships *should* be — sometimes these notions are based on childhood fairy tales, advertising catchphrases, romantic cards, wedding vows, and even catchphrases that you may have bought into: "Two hearts beating as one"; "...and the two shall become one"; "He completes me", "And they lived happily ever after!" and so on. These ideas indeed sound dreamy but they're only part of the story. They don't include the tension between your innate need to be independent while simultaneously needing to be part of a relationship and/or group. (Other clichés such as "Absence makes the heart grow fonder" speak to that very need).

It's all too easy to make assumptions about a new partner or friend based on just a few shared traits. For example, if your new boyfriend likes baseball, pizza and karaoke as much as you do, you may assume that he's like you in many other ways, too, including his core values, political, social, ethical and religious beliefs and even his desire to be a parent one day. And because you like him so much, you want that to be true.

But wanting something to be true doesn't make it so. This is where couples often find themselves at a crossroads later in the relationship. Wishing your partner was more romantic, or dependable, or trustworthy will not make it happen. Within every relationship, there are both possibilities and limitations; one of the things that we aim to accomplish in couple's therapy is that each partner seeks to become all that she or he can become while at the same time accepting that the other partner may *not* become all that is desired.

For partners with unrealistic expectations, this can be difficult to accept. They may feel as though they're settling for less than they want or need or compromising unnecessarily. They may worry that couple's counseling will somehow force them to stay in a relationship that is "not good enough" or that it will convince them to separate even if that's not what they really want. But the actual goal of couple's counseling is just the opposite: instead, it centers on helping each partner find the highest level of fulfillment in the relationship while simultaneously helping develop a greater sense of self — which ultimately leads to less tension and greater satisfaction between partners. The goal is neither to "give in" to the relationship nor "give up" on it.

Of course, in cases where one or both partners is acting out or abusive, those issues must be first addressed before any attention is given to bringing the couple closer together. The same is true for a family undergoing significant stress; when any family member improves her or his own emotional functioning, the whole unit tends to improve in response to that one person changing. This isn't to say the problem necessarily goes away, but it almost always lessens its tightly held grasp on the family. As Dr. Murray Bowen summarized in his family systems theory, this way of looking at family problems provides support for the idea that a) we don't have to change other people to be in a relationship with them, and b) we can be part of a family without being a part of its problems.[16]

When you first meet someone in whom you're interested, it's natural to want to spend a great deal of time with him. You're discovering your mutual interests, perhaps revealing some of your past histories and sort of taking stock of each other's value system and ideology. It's an exciting time in any type of relationship and particularly so in a romantic one. But soon enough, these positive feelings for each other get subsumed by other feelings. You may find yourself feeling jealous that your new love interest goes out to lunch with someone else; or begin to question whether there is hidden meaning behind his every word. Instead of spending your time enjoying the relationship, you focus intently on trying to control the outcome. You may ask yourself, as you have in so many other relationships, "How did I so quickly go from bliss to *this*?"

The answer lies not in fixing the perceived flaws of another person but in being honest with yourself. It takes a great deal of introspection, courage and, yes, hard work to develop a strong basic self that is capable of being an equal partner in any relationship; it's especially challenging for the person who didn't grow up in a family where these things were taught by example. It becomes easier, then, to blame the other person for the problems in a relationship than it is to take accountability. The more you blame, the angrier you become. And the angrier you are, the less likely you're able to work things through logically.

The Elements of a Healthy Relationship

Notice that I'm talking about "healthy" relationships, not "perfect" ones. No person is perfect and so no relationship is either. I believe that any relationship can be improved upon but, as they say, it takes two: two to make it work, two to create conflict, and two to establish healthy or unhealthy patterns.

What you have already learned about your basic self is that in order to feel and get better, you must first fully develop and enlarge that core. And this larger basic self permits better relationships. A healthy relationship starts with two whole people, both of whom have a well-developed basic self, and are ready, willing and able to fully engage in an equal and open exchange. Here are the basics of what that looks like:

- You're able to balance individuality and togetherness,
- You're independent when your partner is not with you (physically or emotionally),

- You know that it's okay to depend on others to a certain degree but that you're also okay on your own,
- You can soothe your own feelings and keep others' opinions and behaviors in perspective,
- You're comfortable knowing the difference between your partner's interests and preferences versus demands, and
- You're authentically yourself in all your intimate relationships.

Recognizing Relationship Patterns

When your sense of basic self is small, you struggle to manage resulting problems. In terms of relationships, you tend to frequently develop conscious or unconscious strategies in an attempt to manage difficulties. Some unhealthy strategies might include projecting our insecurities onto others, playing the blame game, denial, distorted thinking, and so on.

These are just a few of the unhealthy *patterns* that can develop in your relationships — the thoughts, feelings and behavior that keep trapping you. Until you acknowledge the traps that you lay, they remain quite stuck. This explains the tendency to have the same basic argument with your partner, boss, or best friend over and over again.

Though patterns develop in any relationship where open, honest, and emotionally mature communication is lacking, they're heightened in a marriage or romantic partnership. This occurs in large part because of the close physical proximity in the relationship, underscoring the conflict along with the emotional closeness between the autonomous and attached self.

Following are some basic common patterns that Dr. Murray Bowen identified as couples using as ways to try to manage anxiety as a result of trying to be in an intimate or close relationship:[17]

Conflict

Stress or tension that arises when the partners are poorly differentiated, will inevitably find its way into the relationship. Some couples use conflict to manage this stress or tension. There is a cyclical nature to the pattern of conflict. Just about the time a couple moves toward each other, becoming closer and more vulnerable, anxiety in one or both reaches critical mass and boom! They create a fight. The cycle might repeat weekly or monthly or it could be tied to events rather than timing. In its extreme version, conflict in a relationship shows up as physical abuse or violence. Conflict in marriages serves as a distraction for the whole family.

As a side note, one factor that attracts you to both your romantic partner(s) and friends is a similar level of differentiation. If you're poorly differentiated, other-validated rather than self-validated, you will likely find relationships with people having similar concerns. You tend to identify more fully with like-minded people; this is common trait. But what often happens in relationships is that two people who start out with similar levels of differentiation grow in different directions or at different paces. The old adage, "We simply grew apart" becomes true in many cases.

Emotional Distancing

Emotional distancing is the process of one partner emotionally insulating himself from the other. Couples engaged in this pattern will find all kinds of "legitimate" reasons like work, hobbies, volunteer or family commitments to avoid each other. They often avoid being alone as a couple. They may not speak to each other for extended periods of time or have certain subjects that are off-limits. These couples often keep conversations very superficial. In today's world many couples use electronic devices as a way to engage in distancing.

Over and Under-Functioning

People with low levels of differentiation expect either too much or too little from themselves and others. Over-functioning occurs when one partner feels responsible for what the other partner thinks, feels or does, while under-functioning occurs when a partner allows the other person to take responsibility for things he should be thinking, feeling or doing for himself. Two other phrases used to describe this pattern in adult relationships are "parent/child" and "dominant/submissive." Either way, the relationship quickly becomes imbalanced.

Typically, one partner pressures the other to think or act in certain ways and the other yields to the pressure. Both spouses accommodate to preserve harmony but one does more of the accommodating. It can be comfortable for both people — up to a certain point.

The over-functioning person often becomes resentful of carrying more weight in the relationship while the under-functioning person becomes complacent, allowing his partner to take care of him. But he, too, becomes resentful that he is being bossed around, fussed over and treated like a child. He may act out through substance abuse, frequent illness and irresponsible behavior.

This type of relationship pattern isn't limited to couples; it occurs among family members, too. I'm sure you can think of your own examples of a mother who does everything for her children, only to have them do nothing for themselves; or, the husband who keeps important financial information from his wife who "can't handle" potentially upsetting news. Until each partner accepts that he is responsible for himself and only himself in the relationship, tensions will remain high.

Triangles

Another unhealthy way that couples attempt to diffuse anxiety in relationships and create stability is with a triangle. This is when a two-person relationship draws in a third to form a three-person interaction — a triangle. Both partners focus intentionally or unintentionally on the third person (or even a situation) so that they don't have to focus on each other. Triangling includes excessive worry, idealization and even negative views about the third person. The least differentiated person in a family is particularly vulnerable to triangling. In Chapter One, we talked about Sarah moving in with her son Trevor and his wife Kerrie, and how that created a triangle, which became a distraction from the real problem in the couple's relationship, which was lack of honest communication. Sarah was seen as the "problem" in the family. Spreading the tension from two to three can stabilize a system but nothing actually gets resolved.

One example of triangle that I give to clients is the birth of a baby. The very nature of the infant requires his parents' full attention. In baby's first months, the parents naturally talk a lot about his needs, from diapers to feeding and sleeping. *What does this cry mean? Could he be hungry again? Is it too cold to take him outside?* And so on. But it is how quickly the couple can get back to talking about each other rather than just talking about the baby that will determine whether he is a new member of the family or part of a triangle.

Though we often think of triangles in terms of a child or children in a difficult relationship, they're not limited to offspring. Triangles also include a mother-in-law, extreme interest in a pet and even frequent gossiping about someone not in the room. Though triangles are inevitable to some degree in every family, they become a problem when all or most of the couple's time together is spent focused on the third person or situation. An extreme version of a triangle is an extra-marital affair.

Workout

Go back to the genogram you drew in Chapter Two. Now, identify possible relationship patterns within your family system. Who has used these patterns, and what has been the result(s)? What can you learn from them?

Summing Up

Healthy relationships start with healthy people and include taking responsibility for your words, feelings and behavior, setting realistic expectations and practicing open, honest and loving communication. There are no shortcuts but the rewards are immeasurable.

The key to overcoming relationship patterns is to become aware of them. This is one of the values of therapy — to help recognize the use of patterns. Until the root of the problem is fully resolved, things may temporarily improve but tend to revert repeatedly to the original issue. You'll need to learn the skills of "hanging on to self", self-soothing and becoming more open and vulnerable in relationships.

CHAPTER 9

GROWING A BASIC SELF

Meet Your New Best Friend — YOU

As human beings, our greatness lies not so much in being able to remake the world — that is the myth of the atomic age — as in being able to remake ourselves.

- Gandi

By the time you've been in therapy for a while, you're gaining some ideas about where you are in your life and where you want to go. You're beginning to understand that you, and only you, are responsible for yourself, and only yourself, in your relationships. You're becoming more fully aware of the importance of self-soothing. You're also realizing that in order to meet your vital needs, you must first know in very specific terms what those needs are. Now, it's time to focus on growing a basic self. When clients begin to understand that growth requires developing a larger basic self, they almost always ask me, "How do I do that?" The good news is, by showing up for your regular therapy sessions, talking with your therapist, and demonstrating a willingness to challenge your beliefs — you've already planted the seeds. But it goes back to spending a lot of time thinking and reflecting.

Growing a basic self includes incorporating curiosity into your daily life — about yourself, your relationships and the world around you. Knowing who you truly are is essential in determining who you want to be. You can't change who you are until you know who you are. What are your political beliefs? Social beliefs? Your religious affinity, if any? Are you right-brain (intuitive) or left-brain (logical) dominant? Are you artistic or analytical? Patient or impatient? What are your values, morals and priorities? While these things change over time, they tend to do so very slowly; however, who you are and what's important to you at twenty probably isn't the same at forty, at sixty or at eighty.

Children are naturally curious. They unabashedly ask numerous questions about themselves and everything surrounding them (any parent of a two-year old will confirm what I'm saying). On a regular basis, they play in the dirt and try new foods — in these activities, all sorts of interesting answers and preferences are revealed. But as an adult, you tend to forget that it's good and often downright fun to be curious. Instead, you might shame yourself for not already knowing the answer or let logical thinking get in your way.

There are lots of ways to nurture the growing of a basic self:

Pay Attention to Your Vital Needs

Merriam-Webster defines vital signs as "important body functions, such as breathing and heartbeat that are measured to see if someone is alive or healthy."[18] "Vital needs" can be described in much the same way. Of course, vital needs include the basic requirements to stay alive such as food, water, clothing and shelter — and you're fortunate to live in a society where life offers so much more than simply an opportunity to exist. But they include so much more. If you want to *thrive* (as opposed to merely *survive*), you have to include incorporating on a daily basis those vital needs that give you joy, pleasure, gratitude and a sense of peacefulness.

At a early age you develop a set number of vital needs that change very little over time. If you're lucky, you discover at an early age what those needs are and how to ensure they're met on a regular, if not daily, basis. However, if you we come from a dysfunctional family where you weren't taught how to take care of yourself, in an effort to meet those vital needs, you might end up using coping methods that aren't always in your best interests. Substance abuse, compulsive shopping or gambling, overeating and Internet addiction are just a few ways in which people try unsuccessfully to manage feelings in an unhealthy way while neglecting vital needs.

It's easy enough to put off getting your vital needs met, waiting until there is "more time" available. But you need to understand that your present quality of life depends on it. When you feel nurtured, you also experience lower stress levels, less frustration with yourself and your relationships and most importantly, a decreased desire to use inappropriate ways to self-soothe. Make a list of the things that make you feel happy and alive — and then do at least one thing from that list every single day, even if only for a few meaningful moments. Here are some common vital needs and suggestions on how to get them met:

- Personal time — time to do "your own thing." Pursue a hobby, watch TV, go fishing, read, shop, or be involved with an activity unique to you.
- Need to give and do for others — family, community, or your church
- Recognition — for achievement from work, family, or community.
- Movement — daily need for walking, sports, exercise, or shopping.
- Sleep — your day, does not go right unless you have a certain amount of sleep.
- Approval and acceptance — high need for approval and acceptance from coworkers, family, or friends.
- Order and closure - dislike of open-ended situations, tasks, affairs, projects, or goals.
- Time alone — a daily time for reflection and thought while alone.
- Territory — an area of physical space that is your very own.
- Financial security — you want your income and out go always to be in balance. You always want there to be a surplus.
- Being with people — high need for relationships.
- Anticipation — Looking forward to something such as taking a trip or seeing friends. The anticipation is the enjoyment more than the doing.

- Competition — with self, with others, or in sports. High need for challenge.
- Learning something new — acquiring new information is stimulating and exciting to you
- Listening to music — through mechanical means or by playing an instrument
- Having a Project — being creatively involved with ideas for yourself, your home, or community. It provides a feeling of accomplishment.
- Touching — physical contact and touch from and with others is needed regularly.
- Variety of experiences — the need for something new and different going on in your life. High need for change in surroundings, job descriptions, or projects.
- Structured time — schedule and routine are always important. You are uncomfortable when your time becomes too unstructured.
- Unstructured time — you do not like pressure of meeting schedules or having set routines to follow. Generally more creative and love to go with the flow.
- One-on-one attention — desire for relationships to be one on one. May feel stressful when in groups where one-on-one attention is not available.
- Group relationships — need for interaction with groups rather than just one individual.
- Empathy — high need for people important to you, or people around you, to know how you feel, what you are feeling, and the depth of your feelings.
- Humor — the need to laugh and find things funny.
- Spirituality — the need to pursue your beliefs through meditation or fellowship with like-minded individuals.

Are you meeting your own vital needs? If not, how will you begin doing so? If your time or schedule is an issue, can your loved ones help you with that?

While it's unfair to ask someone else to make you happy, it's absolutely fair to ask him to support your own pursuits in doing so.

Workout

> Create a list of your own Vitals Needs. List seven to ten activities or pursuits that give you pure joy, replenishment and/or peace. How often are your needs being met? If your answer is less than daily, it's time to reprioritize your schedule.

Meeting Vital Needs in Relationships

When talking about a relationship — a romance, a friendship or even one that is professional — have you ever thought, "He doesn't make me happy"? Most of us have thought this at one time or another. And it's true that some relationships just aren't meant to be. Call it a lack of chemistry, personality conflict or simply timing. But when you repeatedly find yourself in relationships that "don't make you happy," it may be time to ask yourself — *What does?*

Many of us become aware of our own vital needs only after we find ourselves in an unsuccessful relationship. Or many such relationships. You may still not have clarity regarding what your vital needs are; you only know that the other person isn't meeting them for you. Well, of course not! It's not his job. If you begin a relationship with the expectation that the other person should "make you happy", it's doomed to fail. When you take the time to discover your vital needs, you reclaim your emotional independence. You're now free to enjoy your relationships for what they are — pure expressions of love, companionship and fun — rather than trying to force them to be something they're not.

The most important thing you can do right now to improve any relationship in your life is to commit to improving or further developing your basic self. Take the time to get to know who you really are. Explore and develop your own interests, passions and hobbies. Learn to acknowledge and process *your* feelings before you find yourself, once again, worrying about someone else's. Of course, you cannot put all of your relationships on hold while you figure these things out. Life (and love) goes on. Happily, there is a direct correlation between self- and relationship improvement. As the basic self improves, so, too, will your relationships with others.

Additional Reps

> Go back to your list of Vitals Needs. Now, have your partner and/or family members create their own list(s). Sit down to discuss these needs. Whose needs are being met, and whose aren't? Talk about negotiations so that everyone's Top Seven Needs are being met regularly.

Reading (and more reading)

Reading books on particular subjects that come up in therapy (e.g., boundaries, distorted thinking, etc.) can help you expand on that topic by providing you thorough explanations, examples and step-by-step instructions on implementation. But reading shouldn't be limited to therapy topics. Bibliotherapy (using select books as a means of therapy, or as an adjunct to talk therapy) includes non-fiction and fiction — specifically, where a particular behavior is highlighted and responses to the behavior are an integral story component.

Workbooks

From companion guides that accompany bestselling "self-help" books, to standalone exercises and self-tests — workbooks provide insights, strategies and affirmations that will flex your emotional, intellectual and spiritual muscles between sessions.

Study groups, lectures and workshops

Local colleges and universities present plenty of opportunities to learn from the experts. Also check out offerings from places such as art schools, therapy websites and yoga studios.

Journaling

See Chapter Seven.

Websites

One of the best is the TED website, with instant and free access to a multitude of social and intellectual talks by some of the world's best and brightest. The Khan Academy is another excellent tool; started by a Harvard University and MIT graduate, its stated mission is to provide "a free world-class education for anyone anywhere" on a wide range of topics including math, science, humanities and economics. YouTube is more than just cute kitten videos. It also puts you directly in front of expert lectures and topic-specific musings from the comfort of your own chair. There are hundreds of free courses online (Google search for Massive Online Open Courses or MOOC).

Local Library

Sure, you can check out books (printed and audio) here but many libraries also offer lectures and workshops on a variety of subjects. Plus, how many other places are left in the world where you can hang out for hours in a social setting and learn something new (without having to buy anything)?

Self Help and Support Programs

There are many weekly Twelve-Step Programs for a number of issues including Sex and Love Addicts Anonymous, Alcoholics Anonymous, Recovering Couples Anonymous, Gamblers Anonymous, Eating Disorders Anonymous and many more. There is also SMART Recovery, an alternative support group for addiction recovery, and other types of support groups such as divorce recovery, grief support, living with bipolar and so on.

MeetUp.com

This is a terrific way to find local social groups that get together to network and participate in a variety of interests, from knitting and hiking to tax professionals or a shared loved of Golden Retrievers.

All of the activities, when pursued consistently, are essential components of growing a basic self, which I believe is truly the cornerstone of happiness. Without a strong basic self, your pseudo-self runs the show, leaving us at the mercy of others' whims and opinions. Your goal is to become self-validated rather than other-validated so that you begin to write your own story, rather than living out a story that someone else wrote for you.

Summing Up

Like any other form of growth, growing a basic self takes time, consistent nurturing, patience and thinking but the end result will affect every other aspect of your life in a positive, nurturing way. Have fun with this! After all, you're getting to know the most important person in your life – YOU.

CHAPTER 10

DISTORTED THINKING

It's Not What You Think

Our present perceptions are so colored by the past that we are unable to see the immediate happenings in our lives without distortion and limitations. With willingness, we can reexamine who we think we are in order to achieve a new and deeper sense of our real identity.
-Gerald Jampolsdy, MD, *Love Is Letting Go Of Fear*

"Distorted thinking" refers to the way in which your mind convinces you of something that isn't really true. In the telling of your story over time, you tend to repeat negative thoughts and emotions. At the time of telling, they sound perfectly true and rational but unfortunately, they ultimately perpetuate your stress, anxiety, anger or depression.

In 1980, noted psychiatrist David D. Burns published his work on distorted thinking (also known as cognitive distortions) in *Feeling Good: The New Mood Therapy.*[19] Burns builds on previous findings by his mentor, Aaron T. Beck[20], and lists common distortions and examples of each. In summary, here they are:

- Always Being Right - this need often overshadows your best judgment, and others' feelings.
- Black and White Thinking - also known as "all or nothing" thinking. An example includes statements such as "You always..." or "You never...".

- Blaming - believing that nothing is your fault or similar to personalization, that everything is.
- Catastrophizing – assuming the worst will happen.
- Control Fallacies - external control fallacies leave us feeling controlled by external forces; internal control fallacies leave us feeling responsible for others.
- Emotional Reasoning - believing that if you feel it, it must be true.
- Fallacy of Change - the belief and expectation that others will change to suit our needs.
- Fallacy of Fairness - believing yet not accepting that indeed life is not fair.
- Filtering - highlighting the negative details(s) while glossing over the positive.
- Heaven's Reward Fallacy - expecting (then resenting) the lack of a payoff for self-described "good" behavior.
- Jumping to Conclusions - believing that you know the reason behind the eventual outcome of something before you bother to find out what it will likely be.
- Labeling - attaching an unhealthy label (or judgment) to yourself or another person, based on a prior and potentially unrelated event.
- Overgeneralization - taking one incident and applying it to all incidents.
- Personalization - believing that everything is somehow your fault.
- Shoulds and Shouldn'ts - these speak to the tacit (and often outdated) rules we have created for ourselves, or inherited from our families of origin.

Challenging Distorted Thinking

The first step to overcoming distorted thinking is recognizing it. This is going to take practice both in and out of therapy — lots and lots of practice. You're coming face to face with lifelong habits and initially, challenging them is going to feel weird — perhaps even inauthentic. If you're accustomed to distorted thinking that suggests you're a loser and you suddenly replace it with "I'm a winner!" it won't feel right, at least not initially. That's why it's important to create rational and immediately believable replacements for old, irrational thoughts. For example: Instead of replacing, *"I always fail at new projects; I'm such a loser,"* with *"I succeed at* everything *I do!"* Try, *"I've done very well at some projects while others have been more challenging. I'm persistent and brave enough to take on new things."*

Though there's nothing wrong with telling yourself that you're a winner, for many people taking baby steps toward more rational, less emotional thinking is a necessary first step. In the process, you're learning a new way of thinking that will eventually find its way into your belief system.

Vincent is a highly intelligent man in his thirties who seems to pride himself on being negative. In his family of origin, there was a belief that people who walked around smiling all the time and complimenting others were "phonies" and "Pollyannas." His parents taught him that it was better to be realistic about life than get his hopes up. As a result, Vincent is very adept at certain types of distorted thinking, particularly the "Shoulds and Shouldn'ts" and "Filtering." He admires his father, a history professor, greatly, and has a difficult time imagining that anything he told Vincent during his childhood isn't absolutely true.

The first step for Vincent in overcoming distorted thinking was to write down in his journal his key beliefs that his parents had taught him. Because Vincent is a very analytical type, he needed to break down those beliefs line by line and we discussed them during therapy. Only then was he able to see that just because his dad said something, didn't necessarily make it true for Vincent.

Distorted thinking is often unconscious. Refuting it often involves allowing your unconscious motives to come up into awareness, something that naturally happens over time in therapy. If you can begin to become aware of when and why you engage in distorted thinking, you can better know yourself and think differently.

An example of how this works in therapy is something I do frequently with clients, which is to pay particular attention to and point out the client's choice of words when talking. Words tell both of us what some of the client's distorted thinking is. Vincent might make a statement such as "I didn't do anything fun this weekend. *No one ever* asks me to do *anything* on the weekend." I might point out to Vincent that his choice of words could be the form of distorted thinking we call "Overgeneralization".

Workout

In your journal, write down three repetitive thoughts that keep popping up for you. Are they positive or negative? Are they your words or someone else's, perhaps from your family of origin? Now, look at the types of distorted thinking listed in this chapter. Can you identify which ones you might be using?

How Beliefs Affect Behavior

In 1955, psychologist Albert Ellis developed Rational Emotive Behavior Therapy (REBT), in which he proposed that our beliefs strongly affect our emotional functioning. In particular, irrational beliefs often cause depression, anxiety and anger, which in turn lead to self-defeating behaviors.[21] The Buddha said it best 2,500 years ago: *"All that we are is the result of what we have thought. The mind is everything. What we think we become."*

But what happens when negative thoughts manage to play a loop in your mind? When, no matter how hard you try, you keep coming back to the same distorted thinking? How do you change that?

The answer is first, awareness — and then practice. Substituting negative thoughts with alternatives, on a regular basis, is the only way to stop the self-destructive loop.

It's important, too, to know the difference between a *belief* and a *truth.* The word "belief" means an acceptance that something is true; it does not *make* it true. "Truth" is the confluence of accuracy and logic, whether or not it is your "belief". For example, your mother may have treated you badly, leaving you to believe that were unlovable as a child — but your belief doesn't take into account her own wounds, nor her inability to express love even when she may have felt it. Challenging your belief that you're unlovable doesn't condone your mother's behavior toward you, but it opens you up to the truth: You are lovable, just as you are.

Ellis contended that negative beliefs tend to become "irrational beliefs" — those that seem to attract anxiety and unhappiness. Psychologist Ann Jorn discusses Ellis' theory of irrational beliefs, and summarizes some of them as this:[22]

Core Irrational Beliefs

- Similar to Burns' concept of "shoulds" and "shouldn'ts". For example, *I should be a better dad.* Or, *I shouldn't be so focused on myself.* This leads not only to self-judgment and labeling but also to that of others.
- The idea that everyone needs to love and approve of you (and if they don't, you must change for them or try to control their feelings).
- The belief that you must rely on something or someone greater than yourself to get by.
- The notion that you *must* be successful in all areas and achieve great things (and if you're unable to do so, it will become a huge quality of life issue).
- The idea that there shouldn't be any discomfort in life, which leads to an intolerance for the inevitable disappointment or frustration we will encounter.

Other Forms of Self-Deception

Distorted thinking is typically not intentional but instead is the inevitable result of repeated negative self-talk; nonetheless, when left unchecked it manifests as a form of self-deception. You move beyond actually believing something, to allowing yourself to believe it.

There are several ways to become more fully aware of self-deceptive practices but perhaps the most important is acknowledging your feelings in relation to your words and behavior. If you're embarrassed by something you've said or done, it may be an indication that you've strayed from your core values. Let your conscience be your guide. Don't beat yourself up over it; just use it as a guide for the future. You're developing new tools to keep from making the same painful mistakes.

Taking responsibility for your mistakes makes you grow. It puts you back in the driver's seat. It's far better to admit a mistake with the intention of putting it behind you than to cover it up with the intention of doing it again.

Setbacks are an inevitable part of the process of getting better. It doesn't have to mean one step forward, ten steps back. Problems can be viewed as opportunities to stretch your mind and learn something new.

Learning to deal with uncomfortable feelings is an important component of the therapeutic process. In fact, you may have even begun therapy because you were tired of trying to avoid feelings that are unpleasant, only to have them linger and oftentimes, magnify in their intensity.

Summing Up

Awareness of distorted thinking — what it is and when you use it — is the first step in overcoming it. It's also helpful when you recognize it in your relationships — not as opportunities to judge yourself or others, but realizing that nearly everyone is susceptible to distorted thinking in lieu of what's real.

CHAPTER 11

DEFENSE MECHANISMS

Are They "Evil" or Necessary?

Only in an open, nonjudgmental space can we acknowledge what we are feeling. Only in an open space where we're not all caught up in our own version of reality can we see and hear and feel who others really are, which allows us to be with them and communicate with them properly."
-Pema Chödrön

Dealing with emotional conflict is a lifelong endeavor. Since it's impossible to control the chaotic world around you, the best that you can do is consciously try to minimize anxiety and simply enjoy the moment by learning to manage your thoughts, feelings and behaviors. In other words, you learn to cope. However, you're human and therefore subject to periods of high stress, a bruised ego and feelings of worthlessness. And what else might you do to protect yourself against these things that is *not* so conscious? Enter the defense mechanism.

Unlike coping strategies, the term "defense mechanisms" (first noted by famed psychiatrist Sigmund Freud and discussed throughout his works; later, expanded upon by his daughter Anna Freud)[23] are psychological strategies triggered by the unconscious mind used to repress, lessen anxiety and protect the ego. They're also used to distort reality and triumph over self-labeled or socially unacceptable behavior and impulses.

Though the very phrase "defense mechanism" when used by others to describe your behavior, can make you feel immediately, well, defensive — it's important to note that there are varying degrees of these mechanisms, some of which can be quite helpful to you while others, not so much. Psychiatrist George Eman Vaillant's classification of defense mechanisms is one that is highly useful in understanding more about them. Vaillant expands upon Freud's original classification by grouping them into four basic categories: (1) pathological defense (denial, delusion, depression), (2) immature defense (fantasy, acting out, lying), (3) neurotic defense (displacement, repression, controlling) and (4) mature defense (humor, altruism, sarcasm):[24]

These categories are influenced by emotional health and maturity, as well as by your position on the scale of differentiation. Other defense mechanisms include but are not limited to:[25]

- Agreeing – pretending to agree with someone to avoid conflict. Example: A parent who allows his child to misbehave so he won't pitch a fit in public.
- Affiliation – constantly turning to others for help or support. Example: Seeking advice from others when you're perfectly capable of relying on yourself.
- Avoidance – refusal to engage in situations that cause internal stress. Example: A couple who never has marital fights because the husband avoids his wife's anger.
- Compensation – overemphasizing or over-correcting for perceived flaws or previously encountered failures. Example: The co-worker who buys gifts for everyone in lieu of doing her job.
- Criticism – pointing out another's flaws in deflection of your own. Example: The overweight woman who teases her sister about the size of her hips.
- Deflection – redirecting attention to someone or something else. Example: The employee who changes the subject when asked about a deadline.

- Humor – making jokes in lieu of expressing feelings. Example: The guy who makes fun of his big stomach, joking that he's just "big boned."
- Idealization – placing on a pedestal an object or person of desire. Example: The young woman who thinks her father is a saint for having stayed in an unsatisfactory marriage for many years.
- Indifference – pretending not to care rather than sharing thoughts or feelings. Example: The boyfriend who "forgets" his girlfriend's birthday because he's angry with her.
- Isolation – separating or splitting emotions from thoughts. Example: A person begins to share a train of thought, then changes the subject when he realizes he's sharing too much; he may also talk about a painful incident as if it is someone else's story.
- Minimization – saying or pretending that things are smaller, less important than they are. Example: The wife who says, "It's okay" that her husband missed their anniversary dinner.
- Procrastination – putting things off unnecessarily. Example: Internet shopping when a project is due.
- Rationalization – creating a personally acceptable or logical explanation for something that may not warrant it. Example: A woman says she is better off without her boyfriend when he unexpectedly dumps her.
- Regression – reverting back to past, unacceptable or less desired behavior. Example: Acting like children when adult siblings get together.
- Resistance – a strong opposition to bringing certain thoughts or data into consciousness. Example: Using drugs or alcohol to numb the grief of losing a loved one.
- Running away – removing yourself from a situation rather than dealing with it. Example: "Needing" to run to the convenience store to buy cigarettes during a stressful family gathering.
- Sarcasm – using snarky comments to mask true feelings. "Example: The wife who cuts down her husband because she's frustrated that he doesn't help out around the house.

- Silence – shutting others out by remaining quiet. Example: The teenager who wears headphones 24/7.
- Somatization – the manifestation of unresolved emotional conflict in the physical body. Example: The woman who gets migraines when her in-laws visit.
- Substitution – seeking alternative gratification in the absence of obtaining a desired object (or person). Example: Sexual promiscuity in lieu of finding true love.
- Undoing – a positive act that attempts to negate a prior act with negative connotations. Example: The parent who buys an expensive toy for a child he has shamed.

Becoming Aware of Defense Mechanisms

Defense mechanisms serve to protect your ego when you feel threatened or hurt. However, they also can prevent you from being authentic and vulnerable in your relationships. Furthermore, because they're unconscious, they can be difficult to identify. The easiest way to do so is, whenever you respond to an event or comment in a way that feels a bit contradictory to your gut instinct, simply ask yourself if your behavior might protecting your threatened ego. If so, you may need to spend some time developing your basic self so that you will be less inclined to use defense mechanisms.

Awareness of defense mechanisms and knowing when they are likely to come up is an essential step in overcoming them. They may be put into motion before you even realize it. They become automatic, making it more difficult to be aware of them.

Workout

Create a Defenses Worksheet in your journal. At the top, list a couple of primary emotions that you have difficulty expressing. Perhaps you struggle with anger, fear, pain or even love and joy? In the middle, write down defense mechanisms that you use to avoid these emotions — maybe sarcasm, running away or humor?

Summing Up

When discussing defense mechanisms with clients, I often refer to them as "necessary evils." Another phrase that comes to mind is, "All things in moderation." What I mean by that is, it's natural and necessary to protect your ego with defense mechanisms but overuse results in unhappiness. As you continue building your basic self and raising your level of differentiation, your need for defense mechanisms will decrease.

CHAPTER 12

BOUNDARIES

Respect for Others Begins with Self

Daring to set boundaries is about having the courage to love ourselves, even when we risk disappointing others.
-Brené Brown

You hear a lot of talk about boundaries these days, but just what are they? They are the limits on what you will or won't do or allow with another person. "Boundaries are guidelines, rules or limits that a person creates to identify for themselves what are reasonable, safe and permissible ways for other people to behave towards him or her and how they will respond when someone steps past those limits."[26]

Boundaries help to define your relationships with everyone with whom you interact from the clerk at the post office, to your spouse or partner and to your aging parents. Boundaries determine the level of intimacy you allow yourself with another person and how far away you distance yourself from them; they define your relationship with the world around you. They allow you to be both separate and connected.

Boundaries work in two directions: It's your job to determine how closely you let others in, and also your job to contain yourself so that you don't intrude on someone else's boundaries. The tricky part is, boundaries are different for each person and in each situation. While one person may be entirely comfortable, for example, with hugs from a complete stranger, another may recoil at the very thought.

Boundaries can be too rigid or too loose. A boundary you set for a store clerk is very different than one for a close friend. If too rigid, boundaries shut people out. They may make a person seem distant, aloof or as someone who never asks for help. If boundaries are too loose, you run the risk of getting into inappropriate relationships with others and I'm not talking only about intimate relationships. Talking to strangers about personal things, mistaking sex for love, giving too much of your time and energy, expecting too much from others, become emotionally overwhelmed, saying "Yes" when you really want to say "No" — these are all examples of loose boundaries.

Boundaries should be firm but flexible. They should respect everyone's feelings and thoughts, including your own. When this happens, you're better able to negotiate and compromise ungrudgingly, have empathy, recover easily from emotional hurts and be comfortable with yourself and others.

The four categories of boundaries are:

1. Physical — including personal space, touching, sexual contact, and even things like leaving bathroom doors open during use, or being naked at home in front of children. Think of physical boundaries as those that affect your senses: sight, smell, touch, hearing and taste.
2. Cognitive or Thought — including belief systems, opinions, respecting differences of opinions. An example of cognitive boundaries is when parents hold strong religious or political beliefs and expect their children to hold the same beliefs.
3. Emotional — including lack of emotional control. Some examples include explosive anger or raging, crying uncontrollably in a public place, expecting a child to rescue his parent's emotions, a desire to prevent or manage someone else's emotional breakdown (or expecting the same from others), ridiculing, sarcasm, mocking, abandonment and threat.
4. Spiritual — I'm not talking about religion but instead, referencing those things that violate what feels right to you; spirit killing, name

calling, an assumption that you or another person is "less than" the other, pretending to agree with someone, concealing your true feelings, ignoring your basic and vital needs, and using compulsions and addictions to avoid your feelings.

Another way of classifying is boundaries is in accordance with their strength[27]:

1. Soft - A person with soft boundaries merges with other people's boundaries. Someone with a soft boundary is easily a victim of psychological manipulation.
2. Spongy - A person with spongy boundaries is like a combination of having soft and rigid boundaries. They permit less emotional contagion than soft boundaries but more than those with rigid. People with spongy boundaries are unsure of what to let in and what to keep out.
3. Rigid - A person with rigid boundaries is closed or walled off so nobody can get close to him/her either physically or emotionally. This is often the case if someone has been the victim of physical abuse, emotional abuse, psychological abuse, or sexual abuse. Rigid boundaries can be selective which depend on time, place or circumstances and are usually based on a bad previous experience in a similar situation.
4. Flexible - Similar to selective rigid boundaries but the person has more control. The person decides what to let in and what to keep out, is resistant to emotional contagion and psychological manipulation, and is difficult to exploit.

Workout

In your journal, write down an example of a time when someone came too close to you (physically, mentally, emotionally or spiritually). How did you feel? Now, write about a time when you didn't contain yourself and disrespected someone else's boundary. How did that feel?

In her book on boundaries, Rokelle Lerner uses a popular term when referring to them that resonates with me: "comfort zone". She describes it as "that internal place of sanctuary that we create by developing and maintaining our boundaries" and maintains that, "It's very hard to establish an inner sanctuary if the self is unknown."[28] Bingo! Boundaries, too, center on the basic self. Lerner further states, "[Only when we] claim the totality of who we are...can we experience a state of consciousness that allows us to soothe ourselves with the precious knowledge that we're separate, and yet infinitely connected."[29] In other words, when you know who you are you don't need to fill your time with anxiety about your relationships because you're okay with them — and without them.

Lerner makes an excellent case for boundaries. Why wouldn't you want to establish them in order to more fully enjoy all of your relationships? I believe the answer is, you might not know how. You likely modeled yourself after your family of origin and you may not have witnessed healthy boundaries while growing up. Perhaps you were taught as a child to be polite and deferential in lieu of saying what you wanted or needed. Now, as an adult, you may use desperate means of getting your needs met rather than simply being assertive.

Your boundaries (or lack of them) are the result of what you believe about yourself in the telling of your story. If you believe you deserve respect from others and good things from life, you're more likely to have established healthy boundaries. If you erroneously believe that boundaries are designed to push others back, you will struggle with them. You may even think boundaries are "rude". In truth, they're just the opposite.

Boundaries give you choices, rather than mandates, about how to respond and react appropriately. When they're firmly established, communicated and maintained, there's little need to consistently withdraw from someone who has hurt you; nor is there reason for you to walk on eggshells around a loved one, in fear that you will trigger his negative feelings. It's actually easier to be with someone who has a strong basic self, able to both protect and contain himself by communicating his boundaries in an assertive way.

Resisting Boundaries

The main reason people resist setting boundaries is because they fear it will make someone else feel uncomfortable. If the other person is uncomfortable (hurt, angry, upset), you fear he may not like you or that he may reject or abandon you. If you say to your spouse that you don't like being touched in a certain way or place, you may fear his rejection.

It's true that not everyone is going to embrace your efforts to set boundaries. Some efforts may be met with extreme resistance; some relationships may not work anymore, now that you're no longer willing to sacrifice your integrity. It's going to take courage, determination and consistency on your part to establish new and healthy boundaries. But don't let that stop you; if you give up, your authentic self is at stake.

Boundaries and the Self

In Chapter Three I talked about the components of self and how those play out in your world. When the basic self enlarges, you become self-validated rather than other-validated. You're less focused on what others say and do and more focused on what you say and do. But when the pseudo-self is running the show, you automatically rely on others to validate you. Everything that others do, you're highly affected by so you need to be sure they like you, making it difficult to say or do things that might displease them. It's as though you're blowing with the wind, conforming to the whims of others at your own expense.

Before you can effectively establish new boundaries, you need to spend some time thinking about the things that inform your current boundaries. Are there family rules that no longer apply to you? Perhaps traditions you want to make or break? What are your personal preferences for the way people touch you, or communicate with you? Take a few moments answering the following questions, and in your answers, omit the words "should" and "shouldn't":

1. Do you like hugs? From whom?
2. Are you okay with hugging a co-worker?

3. How do you feel about kissing as a friendly greeting?
4. Do you prefer shaking hands with mere acquaintances, or no physical contact at all?
5. How were you taught to handle criticism as a child? Do you retort with insults, or remain silent?
6. How were feelings expressed among your family of origin? Is it an acceptable form of expression for you now?
7. How do you feel about nudity in your home?
8. Should children be allowed to talk when adults are present?
9. What family traditions (food, culture, relationships) did you inherit? Are they important to you now? What would happen if you let them go?
10. What words or behavior are not allowed in your current home? Are there any you'd like to add, or subtract, to the list?

Once you have a clearer picture of the things that rank high on your own belief system, you will have an easier time thinking of boundaries not as inflexible walls that push others away, but as structural support for your own values and identity.

How do you know when your boundaries have been crossed? Once you have spent more time in therapy becoming familiar with your internal landscape, you will be better at just *knowing*. For many people, it's a feeling in the gut, telling you that something isn't in line with your value system. For instance, if you tend to respond in anger, the sheer fact that you blow up and push someone away is a pretty good indication of a boundary violation, either real or perceived. If you're unaccustomed to responding to a gut feeling (by either minimizing its importance, or employing self-doubt or rationalization), I encourage you to take a step back from a boundary violation and reflect back to the other person what is going on, as you interpret it.

Let's say a co-worker taps you on the head (your pet peeve) while walking past you and says, "The report you turned in yesterday was terrible!" Instead of punching the guy or verbally expressing rage, you could take a deep breath and respond with, "Please don't touch me on the head; if you want to discuss the report, let's schedule a time to do so. This isn't it." In my opinion, the co-worker has committed a fairly significant violation, both physically and emotionally. "Please" would not be included in my response, but I'll leave it up to you to determine what feels right. You've made your boundaries known in a calm but firm way, and your co-worker can respond as he chooses.

Other effective ways of establishing boundaries include:

- "When you/I feel/I'm asking" statements. This means saying something like:

  1. When you ____________________ (e.g., yell at me),
  2. I feel ____________ (e.g., belittled),
  3. So I'm asking you to do _____________ instead."

- Delay statements — when you're uncertain whether or how you want to respond to a question or request, simply say that you will think about it and get back to the other person at a later time. Sometimes you just need time to think and consider how you want to respond.
- Clearly stating what it is that you do want, rather than focusing on or hinting about what you don't want (e.g., *In the future, I would appreciate it if you did* _________).
- Be honest about fears, concerns or discomfort you may be feeling in a situation.
- Consistency and follow-through — be consistent with respect to boundaries, clearly stating the consequences of trespassing, and following through on those consequences when necessary (e.g., *If you do* _____________*, I will confront the behavior and share my feelings. If you continue the behavior, I will* ________________ *to take care of myself*).

Easing Into New Boundaries

Establishing or redefining boundaries doesn't mean that you have to jettison every value that you inherited from your family. Instead, your job is to determine those values which you'd like to keep and those which no longer work for you. Then, your values become not hand-me-downs but choices that allow you to respond to others' boundary intrusions in a conscious manner, rather than reacting to them with emotional turmoil.

Here are a few things to keep in mind as you set healthier boundaries, modified from *Boundaries: Where You End and I Begin* by Anne Katherine:[22]

- It's okay and perfectly natural to feel a bit selfish or guilty when setting a healthy boundary. You're doing something important to take care of yourself. As boundaries become second nature, these feelings will dissipate.
- You cannot set a boundary and at the same time, be responsible for someone else's feelings. If that person disrespects your boundary, you're probably better off without them.
- Be respectful when setting a boundary, but be firm. If you waver, you're sending a mixed message and others won't take you seriously.
- Anger, frustration and resentment are all good indications that a boundary needs to be set.

Summing Up

Like any type of change, learning to set new boundaries takes time. Sometimes it feels uncomfortable; even downright painful. But when you know yourself, you know that any change you make that is congruent with your values is not only desired but also essential to your well-being. Honor the process, allow it to happen as it does and most importantly, be patient and loving with yourself.

CHAPTER 13

COMMUNICATION

Ready to Talk — with Others

If someone comes along and shoots an arrow into your heart, it's fruitless to stand there and yell at the person. It would be much better to turn your attention to the fact that there's an arrow in your heart...
-Pema Chödrön, *Start Where You Are: A Guide to Compassionate Living*

One of the most frequent complaints couples bring to my office is lack of communication. When talking about communication, you probably think of verbal exchanges — the conveyance of information and news that keeps you connected with others. But communication is so much more than verbal. You can communicate with words, silence, gestures, behaviors and expressions. It's putting your thoughts and feelings out into the world and has a considerable impact on all of your relationships. It affects the way that others view you and the way in which you view yourself.

Babies and toddlers naturally convey their feelings and "ask" for what they need. If they're happy, they laugh. If they're sad or hungry, they cry until their needs are met. You were actually born to be an assertive communicator. But as you grew and learned to experience both joy and disappointment, you may have begun to realize that life and communication are more complicated than "ask and ye shall receive." Perhaps you communicated your needs to your family but those needs weren't met. Or, open communication was discouraged. Instead, you may have witnessed countless examples of passive or aggressive communication styles, or a combination of both. As a result, either you're struggling to effectively communicate to meet your own needs or, just the opposite, you use it less as a tool and more as a weapon for whipping others into compliance.

Communication can be direct or indirect, verbal or nonverbal. These days, it's often done over the phone, or by email or text. Sometimes, relationships are impacted more significantly by what's *not* said than by what is. Imagine someone responding to your grief with a simple hand on your shoulder; how comforting that might feel. Imagine, too, someone rolling his eyes at you when telling him you're hurting.

How do you currently communicate your thoughts and feelings? Are you quick to share them with others, rarely using a filter when choosing your words? Perhaps you're more reserved, letting only a select few in on what's going on inside you? Do you "say what you need to say" (as John Mayer sings it) or have frequent regrets about the things you didn't?

Communication Styles

Passive

Passive communication styles often emanate from a person with a poor sense of basic self. He may believe that by withholding what he's thinking, he's keeping the peace but then he's also allowing resentment and anger to build up. Because he's often unaware or in denial of his own feelings, he's able to convince himself that "he isn't really angry" or that another person's offensive comment or behavior "wasn't such a big deal". His boundaries are typically permeable and his speech is often peppered with apologies.

Because the passive communicator rarely stands up for himself, he tends to attract aggressive friends who take advantage of him. They're looking for someone to control and he allows himself to be controlled.

When the passive communicator has finally reached his limit with others stepping on him, he will often have a blow-up of epic proportions. Witnesses are left wondering, *I wonder why he got so upset over something so small?* He frequently feels alienated from others and powerless.

Aggressive

Aggressive communication style checks the proverbial box for "know how to stand up for yourself" but fails to check the box underneath it that says "...but not at the expense of others." Aggressive communication violates the rights of others, ultimately creating anger and resentment rather than respect. Like passive behavior, it stems from low self-esteem but manifests instead in over-compensation. It becomes sort of a game of "whomever yells the loudest, wins the argument."

The aggressive communicator tries so hard to convince others that he is right, or superior, or entitled, he fails to realize that others run when they see him coming. This communication style often comes from the need to control others or outcomes.

Passive-Aggressive

Passive-aggressive communication is a style that combines the appearance of the passive communicator's non-combative style with the "in it to win it" style of the aggressive communicator.

How can you exhibit both styles simultaneously? Easy: Smile when you're really angry, tell someone that he didn't hurt your feelings when he did (then refuse to answer his calls), deny problems when confronted, and appear to be cooperative when you're not. You hide your motives, then proceed to sabotage others behind their backs. A good example is agreeing to meet someone for coffee when you don't really want to, then showing up fifteen minutes late.

The passive-aggressive communicator typically believes that he's very good at smoothing things over, but often ends up alienating others because he's not honest with them or himself.

Assertive

Assertive communication is emotionally intelligent. It means standing up for your rights without infringing on others'. Unfortunately, many of us (particularly girls) are taught as children that assertive behavior and aggressive behavior are the same. They're not.

Assertive communication includes clearly and directly stating feelings and opinions while allowing others to do the same. The assertive communicator, unlike the other three styles, feels mostly connected to others because he's not trying to manipulate anyone and because he places a high priority on getting his own emotional needs met.

Looking at these four communication styles begs the question, *Wouldn't there be fewer relationships problems if everyone practiced assertive communication?* And the answer is, *Yes!* But the most likely reason you've avoided assertive communication in the past is that you simply didn't know how to do it. Assertive communication style can definitely be both learned and improved upon, but it's also tied to your awareness of basic self, your level of self-esteem, your ability to set healthy boundaries, your level of differentiation, and your respect for others' opinions and feelings.

Better Communication for Individuals

Effective communication skills for any individual involves first, knowing who you are and knowing your basic self. You must have a good sense of what you like or don't like, what makes you tick or pushes your buttons, what your priorities and your core values are and also, how you feel most comfortable when interacting with others. We all know a person (or two) who says very little in public but if you receive a letter or email from him, are astounded by how much he has to say in written form. You also probably know someone who loves being in the limelight and never stops talking but if you try chatting with him one-on-one, he'll clam up.

How do *you* prefer communicating with others? Are you at ease in small groups or large? If a difficult conversation is going to take place, would you prefer it be verbal or written? Knowing your communication comfort zone and working whenever possible in that zone gives you a sense of autonomy. Acknowledging your feelings and understanding your preferences means that you can better convey those things to others. To be sure, it's impossible to communicate what you don't know, or what you won't allow yourself to feel.

Practice Becoming an Assertive Communicator

When you have a good sense of your basic self — including your thoughts, feelings and opinions — and you honor those things every single day, you'll automatically be a more assertive communicator. But if you're still working on developing your basic self, there are several ways in the meantime to practice being a more assertive communicator; sort of a "fake it 'til you make it."

It's true that you can't control everyone around you. You can control only yourself. So, when others don't behave the way you wish they would, you're entitled to express your disappointment but you're not entitled to call names, lay blame, or throw a hissy fit in an attempt to manipulate them. You can *try* doing these things, but I guarantee you won't be happy with the results. If you scream at a friend who's always late, it's likely to escalate to a much bigger issue.

Instead, try the following:

1. Switch to "I" statements. State what the problem is, how you feel about it, and how you would prefer the situation to be. For example:

   "When you're late, I feel hurt and angry. I worry that something bad has happened to you or, that my time isn't valuable to you — or both. I prefer that you be on time, or at least let me know when you're running late."

2. Get comfortable with silence. Not every moment needs to be filled with words. Silence performs some heavy lifting in difficult conversations; it allows you to process what the other person has said and it signifies to them that you're ready to listen.

3. Speak clearly, maintain eye contact (without staring the other person down) and be aware of your body language. Are you unconsciously making yourself appear smaller or larger?
4. Avoid ambiguity. Know what you want ahead of time, and what you want to ask for. Let the other person decide how he would like to respond and whether he can honor your requests.
5. Know when to apologize and when to avoid unnecessary apologies. Don't use words that minimize your feelings.
6. Be a good listener. If the other person's words are starting to press your buttons, take a moment to repeat back what the other person is saying. For example:

   "What I'm hearing from you is that you don't really care for dogs in general, and my dog's barking is particularly annoying to you."

7. Ask questions. Hearing someone else's viewpoint allows you to have a deeper understanding of the situation and the person, which often leads to reframing your own viewpoint and/or more compassion. Ask questions like,

   "Why do you think that happened?"
   "How did you feel about it?"
   "What do you wish had happened?"

8. Be aware of physical sensations (shortness of breath, a pit in your stomach) and if it's getting to be too much for you, it's okay to take a break and finish the conversation at another designated time.
9. Take responsibility for your words and actions but not those of others. Allow them to do that for themselves.
10. Acknowledge other people's feelings. This doesn't necessarily mean you have to feel the same way, or even that you have to agree with the other person's side of the story but feelings are feelings and it's important to allow others to express them, just as it's important to express your own.

Better Communication for Couples

Effective communication between couples requires both self-respect and mutual respect. When you fully understand that our feelings are just feelings, then you're better able to grasp that your partner's feelings are the same. You no longer feel obligated to take others' feelings and opinions so personally.

Psychologist John Gottman has extensively researched couples' relationships and determined that there are four highly destructive communication patterns that if repeated over time, can lead to major problems, if not breakups. He calls these patterns the "Four Horsemen of the Apocalypse" (a Biblical reference to the four precursors of ultimate destruction). The Four Horsemen are:[30]

1. *Criticism* – Attacking (or chipping away) your partner's personality, habits, words, appearance, etc. Criticism often begins with the simple word, "You…" as in, "You're so cheap," or "You're just like your father." "You" statements have the ability to quickly undercut anything that may otherwise be going well in a relationship.
2. *Contempt* – Assuming that you're better than your partner; looking down on him in a way that is meant to insult. Contempt includes verbal communication like name-calling and mockery, and non-verbal methods such as smirking and eye rolling.
3. *Defensiveness* – Refusing to hear your partner out or to take any responsibility for problems in the relationship. Defensiveness is often riddled with excuses and cross-complaining or cross-blaming ("I wouldn't have been late if you hadn't distracted me").
4. *Stonewalling* – Silence, withdrawal, subject changing and one or two word answers are typical examples of stonewalling. Partners who engage in this practice think they're "playing it safe" — in other words, they believe that if they say nothing in response to their partner's concerns, they can't get into much trouble. But stonewalling often has just the opposite effect because partners feel shut out, disapproved and disconnected from them.

If you recognize yourself or your partner as one or more of the Four Horsemen, take action. Gottman's research reveals that when these communication patterns are chronically present in any relationship, they're almost doomed to fail.[31] As always, start with yourself. Commit to regularly practicing the assertive communication tips already listed in this chapter, and to those, add these:

1. Practice loving-kindness. Whenever you're tempted to complain to or about your partner, ask yourself this question: *Is it better to be right or kind?*
2. Give compliments daily. Make them authentic — if your partner is bit of a slob, don't tell him you appreciate his neatness. But you can tell him you love that he brings you coffee every morning. Even if he brushes them off, I guarantee you that *everyone* likes to hear something nice about himself.
3. When your partner shares a concern with you, let him talk. And while he's talking, shift your inner dialogue from one of, "I suppose you're blaming me for this!" to "He's just sharing his feelings with me. I'm going to hear him out before I respond."

Even relationships between people with fairly well developed differentiation sometimes hit bumps in the road; bumps that can be smoothed with better communication skills. When you get very familiar with another person, you may also get complacent. You assume that he knows your feelings or that you know his. You then make assumptions about his actions based on your perceived notions of his feelings. Then you act on your assumptions based on your perceived notions of his feelings. See how complicated this can get?

Wouldn't life be infinitely easier if you expressed your own feelings and really listened to your partner when he shared his? In intimate relationships, communication needs to be shared 50/50 — this includes listening and talking as well as being authentic, vulnerable and openly curious about internal experiences.

Creating Safety

Communication isn't going to happen if people don't feel emotional safety. Creating safety is an important aspect of good communication. Here are a few ideas:

- Ask for a specific time to have important, serious conversations. For example, *"I have something important I'd like to share with you. Can we make some time to do that this evening?"*
- Make eye contact.
- No TV's, cell phones or other devices.
- Keep in mind the "5-1 Rule" — to compensate for one criticism, you must offer five statements of appreciation.

Effective Listening Skills

Clearly expressing your feelings, needs and wants in a mutually respectful way is an important part of a healthy relationship but let's not forget about the other half of communication: Listening. Being an effective listener can be challenging; when your partner is talking, you may be tempted to jump in with your own "helpful" suggestions or summaries when the other person really just wants to be heard — really heard.

Here are some tips that you can incorporate in your daily communication with your partner or really, anyone with whom you wish to enjoy improved communication:

- You have the right to remain silent. Use it! Your partner is telling you something he wants you to know. Though you probably have at least some sort of an opinion about what he's saying, make the decision to refrain from sharing it at this time. Focus instead on being an attentive listener.
- Listen for *emotions* that he's sharing with you as he talks, or emotions that he's not sharing. Trying seeing things from his point of view.

- Listen for *values* that he's communicating to you. If he says, "You're spending too much time at work rather than at home," he's communicating that he values spending time together.
- Listen for *beliefs* that he's conveying.
- Reflect back what he's telling you to show him that you're trying to understand him: *So what you're saying is, at that moment, you felt very frustrated,* etc. and also ask him, *What is it that you're telling me now that is important to know or understand?*
- Thank your partner for sharing with you.

Initially, the conversations may end with "thank you for sharing that with me" — and that's it. But over time, as you and your partner develop better communication skills, you'll both probably feel more comfortable in taking the conversation to a deeper level.

Better Communication for Families

Families have all sorts of potential challenges when it comes to communication. For some, it may include blending new family members following a divorce/remarriage. For others, it's more about teenagers who stop talking to parents because, well, they're teenagers. Perhaps a child in the family has suffered emotional or physical trauma and as a result, has difficulty expressing his feelings. Still other families don't communicate effectively because they haven't had any help or practice in doing so.

Workout

Schedule a "feelings meeting." For couples, take turns (every other day) where one person shares his feelings and the other listens. Go through the list of primary feelings and share an experience having that feeling over the last few days. For example, *I felt sad when ________; I felt joy about ____________*, etc.

For families, everyone gets a turn sharing his primary feelings or, each person can take just one feeling each day and share that.

If you're in family counseling, you're no doubt discussing feelings during many sessions. But there are additional ways to practice healthy, assertive communication between sessions. Start by scheduling weekly, short (five to ten minutes) "Feelings Meetings" as suggested above. You can also use conversation starter cards (my office sells them) that prompt participants to open up a dialogue about a fun or even not-so-fun memory or preference. Questions might include, "What was (or will be) the scariest thing about leaving home?" or "What's your favorite time of the day, and why?"

Whether it's a couples or family feelings meeting, in either case, the listener(s) practices active listening skills in which he is attentive and engaged but refrains from comment or trying to "fix" others' feelings. Initially, he just listens. After a month or so of practicing this skill, he may choose to comment a bit or talk more about what he hears.

The listener should consider his job an important one. He is creating a vessel that will hold important information that is shared with him. But just as a real vessel can be a beautiful work of art, it can also develop holes, or become too full, or not full enough. The listener is asked to put his own story up on a shelf for a while in order to hear the other person. It's sort of like closing the chapter of a book, to be re-opened at another time.

Being an active listener with the ability to both set and respect healthy boundaries lends itself to more open, honest and rewarding communication with loved ones.

Better Communication for Conflict Resolution

No matter how skilled a communicator you are, you're bound to have conflict in your relationships. The conflicting desire to be alone and also attached to others has built-in room for potential problems. Here are some tips to keep in mind when conflict arises:

- Remember to use "I" statements ("I feel sad when you forget my birthday") that allow you to express your feelings rather than "you" statements that assign blame.
- Time-outs aren't just for kids – if you and your partner or family member are getting particularly worked up, take a little break and do something quiet or relaxing, alone. It's a good idea to agree in advance to take time-outs so that nobody feels abandoned during a conflict.
- Focus on the problem at hand, not on the person. Avoid insults, name-calling or mocking. These things are often remembered far longer than the actual conflict, and they aren't productive.

Disagreement is a natural part of a relationship. So the question is not, *How can my loved ones and I avoid disagreements* but instead, *How can we work through disagreements?* The answer lies in a commitment toward better communication.

Summing Up

Good communication skills involve clearly stating what you want in a mutually respectful way but don't forget about the other side of the coin: Being a good listener. When you practice good listening skills, it's as though you are creating a sort of important vessel in which to safely store the other person's information. On the other hand, when you are a careless listener it's as though the vessel becomes a trash bin, ready to discard what someone else thought important enough to share.

Try your best to listen with the intent of understanding the person who is talking to you rather with than the intent of replying. It will change your life.

CHAPTER 14

IT'S COMPLICATED

Setbacks, Obstacles and Stumbling Blocks

An obstacle can be either a stepping stone or a stumbling block.
It's your choice.
-Author Unknown

Even if you've done the work, as we say, and made significant progress with the help of therapy — and I trust that you have — there are bound to be setbacks, obstacles and stumbling blocks. These things are inevitable, making life and therefore therapy more complicated. But when you're realistic about complications, you can accept them more easily — as part of the therapeutic process and also life in general. The key to dealing with them in the healthiest way possible is to learn how to cope with them and not let them defeat you. As has been said, "The only way out is through."

Let's say that a person has been very successful on a weight-loss plan when the holidays roll around; he knows that this is the only time of the year that he gets to sample his elderly grandmother's delicious cooking. Does this mean he has to suffer while his family eats with abandon all around him? No! It just means that he needs to have an advance plan — a strategy — for enjoying himself while staying on course. He can walk for an extra hour the day of the big family meal, or perhaps he can decide to have just a few bites of everything granny offers. He could have a light breakfast that day, saving his calories for the big feast. In other words, he has lots of sensible options when it comes to challenges and so do you. Let's look at common stumbling blocks:

Shame and Guilt

In a TED talk on the subject of shame, research professor and noted author/speaker Brené Brown calls shame a "web of unobtainable, conflicting, competing expectations about who we're supposed to be." She defines it as a basic "fear of disconnection" from others. You may think about shame in terms of feeling bad about something that you've done, but shame is more about who you are.[32]

While *guilt* focuses on your behavior, *shame* speaks directly to your sense of worthiness or lack thereof. You're more likely to experience shame if your basic self is underdeveloped and almost certainly if you have experienced violations of love and safety.

Many of us compare ourselves to others on a regular basis, concluding that we don't measure up. Shame is shrouded in thoughts such as, "If they only knew who I really am," and "Why would she want to spend time with me?" You may hide these thoughts from others because you believe that your secrets keep you safe but in truth, they isolate you.

All humans are vulnerable to feelings of shame, at least from time to time. But what if you spend an excessive amount of your time feeling shame? Feelings of shame can do a real number on self-esteem and the ability to truly connect with others. It can also create and magnify self-doubt even in areas where you've worked very hard to improve.

While you're developing your basic self, you can still manage feelings of shame by reframing them in a more positive way. Use these daily affirmations to counteract feelings of both shame and guilt:

I express my truth.
I trust my instinct of what I know is right.
I am grateful for who I am and release any guilt.
I release the hurts of the past; all is well.
My intentions are a blessing; there is no blame.

Forgiveness

I'm sure you've heard about the importance of forgiving — both yourself and others; it's an essential part of putting unfortunate incidents behind you and moving forward with an open heart. Yet, knowing about forgiveness and actually putting it into practice are different. Forgiveness requires honesty, accountability (as opposed to blame) and acceptance of the facts.

Forgiveness does not condone an infraction against you but it recognizes the possibility of human error and includes a firm commitment to letting it go. True forgiveness takes place whether or not a formal apology is made (and often times, there is no such apology, no matter how much you hope for it). It's almost certain that if you can't forgive your own mistakes, you will struggle forgiving others'. Begin the act of forgiveness with yourself, using these daily affirmations:

I forgive myself and others.
I easily forgive, and am easily forgiven.
Forgiveness is part of healing my past.
I offer forgiveness without expectations.
Mistakes are important lessons; I forgive all mistakes.

Many people find it helpful to have a visual cue when using these affirmations, such as putting a marble or button in a jar for each one recited, and adding to it each day. By the end of a month, you'll see the cumulative effect of practicing forgiveness and hopefully, feel it as well.

Workout

One of the exercises I recommend is called "Regrets, Requests and Appreciation." In your journal, draw three vertical columns, one for each category. In the left column, write down the things you have done that you believe were harmful to either yourself or a loved one. In the middle column, include what you want from loved ones to improve your relationship with them and in the right column, jot down the traits and behaviors of your loved one that you like and admire. This exercise is helpful in a number of areas but especially so regarding forgiveness and communication.

If you're struggling with forgiveness, it may be because you're still focusing on whose fault something is — either your own or another person's. A particular client named Jacob comes to mind. When I met him, he was still very angry with his ex-wife who'd left him five years earlier. We talked about how Jacob needed to take responsibility for his own role in creating the relationship they had rather than on his wife's choice to leave. This helped Jacob move closer to forgiveness.

Responsibility

Life is complicated. Humans are complicated. Most people are not out to hurt you or "get you." Rather, they make choices in their behavior in order to get their own needs met; and you are sometimes hurt in the process. It helps to understand that others are not "doing it *to you*; they're just doing it."

Blame is very easy to assign and sometimes difficult to distinguish from responsibility. When you insist on blaming, you're viewing the world in black and white terms (i.e., everything *has* to be either "my fault" or "your fault"). You also invite a whole host of other complications including a tendency toward extreme perfectionism, irrational beliefs, negative thinking patterns and denial.

Responsibility, on the other hand, is not about blame but about identifying and accepting actions and their consequences. Though responsibility is a healthier alternative to blame, emotionally speaking, it's not necessarily something that is taught with reverence in many families. In fact, some family systems see the person who takes responsibility as weak or passive; it's better to end a disagreement by cutting off a relationship with a loved one than by admitting "defeat" with an apology.

As an adult, if you continue the blame game rather than learning to accept responsibility, you begin to see it playing out in your relationships. A relationship simply cannot sustain itself if you always have to be "right" and the other person is invariably "wrong."

A couple may come to me for help with communication problems but in truth, each partner spends time blaming the other. Instead of really listening to each other and accepting responsibility for themselves, they're focusing on what the other person is doing wrong. As a result, they're in a defend/blame cycle and unable to make progress in their relationship. Would you rather be right or *happy*?

Addiction

While addiction — whether it involves food, alcohol, drugs or behavioral patterns — is technically a disease in itself, it's also often a symptom of deep, unacknowledged or unresolved shame. At its core, addiction can develop from seeking a "quick fix" or temporary coping method for dealing with vulnerability, but it's anything but a fix or a cure. In fact, it has just the opposite effect of healthy self-soothing techniques; instead of meeting our vital needs, addiction creates a bottomless need for *more.*

Addiction, if left untreated, will undoubtedly create numerous stumbling blocks on your path to an improved, happier and less anxious existence. Though addiction allows you on some level to numb your pain and decrease our discomfort, it also lessens your capacity to experience real joy and authenticity.

Are you wondering whether you have an addiction? Here are some common signs that may indicate a substance problem:

- Do you use (food, drugs, alcohol, destructive behavior) to distance yourself from or escape your home or work life?
- Does your behavior affect you and/or your family's welfare?
- Does it affect your financial security?
- Do you hide your behavior from loved ones?
- Do you lie about it?
- Are you usually alone when you engage in the behavior?

- Has the frequency of your behavior increased in recent months?
- Do you struggle with memory loss as a result of drinking or drug use, and/or do you have difficulty remembering how much you ate or spent?
- Do you take unnecessary risks to accommodate your behavior?
- Is your behavior affecting your reputation and/or have loved ones expressed their concern about it.

If you're struggling with addiction or suspect that you might have a problem, don't hesitate to discuss it with your therapist who will help you decide an appropriate treatment plan.

Difficult Personalities

Personality disorders (also known as "PDs") are not exactly representative of mental illness, *per se*, but they're psychological conditions that can dramatically affect people's lives. PDs are mental disorders that are characterized by a chronic, inflexible, and maladaptive pattern of relating to the world.

According to the American classification of psychiatric disorders called the DSM-V,[33] personality disorders fall into the following three broad types (though it's important to note that these characterizations are based largely on observation, and multiple PDs often blur into each other in the same person):

Odd, bizarre, eccentric – including paranoid (distrusting, suspicious, withdrawn), schizoid (no desire or capability for relationships) and schizotypal (obsessions, magical thinking, paranoia) behaviors.

Dramatic, erratic – including antisocial (disregard for others and their feelings), borderline (such as bipolar affective disorder), histrionic (seductive, manipulative) and narcissistic (strong need to admire one's self and be admired) behaviors.

Anxious, fearful – including avoidant (based on perceived or anticipated rejection), dependent (strong need to be taken care of by others) and obsessive-compulsive ("my way or the highway") behaviors.

Dealing with a PD (yours or someone you know) is a challenge, to be sure. In order to make much progress, PDs require long-term therapy and a solid commitment to trying to understand associated behavior. If you're in a relationship with someone who has a PD, it's important to acknowledge that you may be enmeshed in his problem. If that person is your parent, partner or child, you've very likely spent a great deal of time trying to figure out what *you're* doing wrong; how *you're* somehow provoking his behavior.

When you have a better understanding of the nature of PD, you realize that you, in fact, aren't causing the problem. However, you may have been contributing to it because you were previously unaware that the PD existed. I call PDs the "crazy makers" because no matter how diligently you try to work around another person's PD, you'll be unsuccessful. You can't wish, or love, a PD away.

Much of what I'm saying is based on the assumption that a person with a PD has been formally diagnosed, when in fact many people with PDs believe they don't have a problem (which is part of the problem!) and refuse to seek professional help. I don't want to encourage you to start diagnosing difficult personalities in your life because not all difficult personalities are disorders. (Even if a person does not have a PD, he may nevertheless display several characteristics of one.) However, if you have at least a general understanding of certain traits and behaviors associated with PDs, you're better prepared to respond to them in a proactive way and also to recognize any of those traits in yourself.

The good news for you is that by employing what you're learning through therapy and this book, you'll come to a place where you can emotionally separate yourself enough from a person with a PD so that you don't get entangled in his dysfunction. The more adept you are at distinguishing your beliefs and feelings from his, the better able you are to make healthy choices when dealing with him.

A well-developed basic self, including boundary setting, rational thinking, the ability to express thoughts and feelings, as well as the ability to heal from any damage caused by being in a relationship with a difficult personality, are all things that will help you when dealing with a person with PD. But you also need to understand that the level of intimacy you can achieve with that person is almost always limited by his psychological condition.

Mood Disorders

While many people are occasionally affected by short-term episodes of "the blues" mood disorders are more serious. They can be persistent or chronic and have a significant impact on a person's quality of life. The two major categories of mood disorders are:

- *Depressive disorder* (including clinical depression and major depression)
- *Manic depression/bipolar disorder* (marked by moods that periodically swing from elation or severe irritability to moderate or severe depression)

There are subcategories of these disorders, however, that are sometimes overlooked: *Disthymic disorder* is a milder form of depressive disorder, and *Cyclothymic disorder* is a milder form of bipolar disorder. While symptoms are typically less dramatic than those of the major mood disorders, they still have the capacity to be debilitating. In order to be diagnosed as a disorder, symptoms must be present most of the time, for at least a two-year period.

Mood disorders are not only emotional stumbling blocks; they can also affect a person's physical health. If left untreated, *depressive disorder* has been linked to heart disease, certain types of cancer and diabetes. Sleeping and eating patterns are often disrupted (placing additional stress on the body) and relationships typically suffer. *Manic depression/bipolar disorder* can affect a person's decision-making abilities, sex drive, and energy level in profound ways — sometimes leading to destructive behavior patterns and an increased level of denial.

If you're dealing with your own mood disorder, it's very important that you receive proper diagnosis and treatment. Talk therapy that includes both individual and family counseling, as well as mood-stabilizing medications and anti-depressants (for those who tolerate them well), offer promising results for mood disorders. Your therapist will typically refer you to a primary medical doctor or psychiatrist, and the two will work together to monitor the effects of your medication. There are several additional ways in which to manage mood disorder symptoms:

- Know what your particular stressors are (both individual and in relationships) and avoid them. These include stressful situations and any foods, drugs or alcohol that affect mood.
- Include regular exercise into your routine. Many people with mood disorders get good results from mind-body connective exercises such as yoga or tai chi.
- Incorporate a daily mindfulness/spirituality practice such as meditation, prayer, journaling and deep breathing.
- Join and interact with support groups.
- Get proper rest and nutrition.
- Develop better coping tools for stress management.

Trauma and Post Traumatic Stress Disorder (PTSD)

In therapy, when we talk about trauma, we typically classify it as "Big T" trauma and "Little t" trauma: "Big T" might include abuse (physical, mental or emotional), rape, death of a loved one, military service (particularly combat), surviving a major natural disaster such as a tornado, hurricane or house fire and surviving a major accident (car, sports-related, etc.); "Little t" trauma includes anything else.

Both types of trauma deserve attention. Though "Big T" trauma may be easier to recognize because of its magnitude, recovery is often more difficult. "Little t" trauma on the other hand may be easier to move past, but the fact that it's often *not* recognized or acknowledged means that its effects can linger for years — thereby hindering emotional progress and leaving its victim wondering why he is "stuck."

You have both cognitive and emotional memories. For example, when you walk into a home that smells just like your grandmother's house. Before you even have a cognitive thought about it, you may experience an emotional memory. That memory may be pleasant (if grandma loved you dearly and always made your favorite cookies) or highly unpleasant (if she treated you badly and her house always smelled like a certain perfume). Another example includes the trauma associated with childhood sexual abuse or rape; until it's acknowledged and dealt with, it's very common to experience an emotional reaction to any type of sexual intimacy as an adult--even in a healthy and loving relationship.

Though talk therapy is an integral part of the healing process for victims of trauma, there are other specific therapies designed to help, including:

- *Eye Movement Desensitization and Reprocessing* (EMDR) – used to alleviate the symptoms of severe unresolved trauma. The goal of EMDR is to help process the emotions surrounding a traumatic event, reduce the anxiety associated with it, and provide adaptive coping mechanisms.
- *Hypnotherapy* – used to retrain the subconscious mind's perceptions and beliefs; in this case, in relation to the traumatic event.
- *Experiential therapy* – a form of therapy that helps identify subconscious issues through experiences including the use of props, role-playing and guided imagery. Experiential therapy includes art therapy, music therapy and play therapy (often used to help children) and letter writing to the perpetrator (or perhaps the parent who did not protect the victim). It's important to note that with letter writing to the perpetrator, you will want to discuss it first with your therapist, especially if you're planning to send the letter.
- *Therapeutic letter writing* – this type of letter writing incorporates the "inner child" to look at unresolved childhood experiences whose consequences linger into adulthood. This type of letter is typically not written with the intention of sending. You begin writing a letter to your child self, first telling him how special he is. You can include details about what he liked to do at a particular age and how much he means to you. Then, express how you feel about him, and how you feel that his needs were not met at such a tender age. Finally, tell him how you will take care of him in the future and how much you love him now. Therapeutic letter writing is an opportunity to re-parent yourself, and it can be a powerful healing exercise.

Anxiety

Anxiety is one of the most common disorders in the United States, but many people are reluctant to talk about it. Yet left untreated, anxiety takes front and center of other issues that need to be addressed. It's difficult to get a handle on healing old wounds when you're dealing with anxiety on a regular basis.

There are many tools that can help manage anxiety including:[34]

- Medications including antidepressants (particularly SSRIs) and benzodiazepines such as Xanax, Valium and Ativan
- Changing the brain using repetitive behavior and thoughts
- Meditation
- Listening to soothing music
- Finding a "happy place" (a tranquil vision)
- Surrounding yourself with a calm environment
- Breathing exercises
- Monitoring caffeine levels

Clinical Depression

The same is true for depression as anxiety. Managing it is key to your success in the therapeutic process. Here are some options:

- Medications including antidepressants (particularly SSRIs)
- Exercising
- Spending time in nature
- Proper nutrition
- Monitoring alcohol and drug use

Attention Deficit Disorder (ADD)

I can't tell you how many times over the years couples have come to me seeking help for their relationship and after spending just a few hours together it becomes painfully obvious that one of the partners has a severe case of untreated attention deficit disorder (ADD). ADD is characterized by:

- Persistent short attention span
- Distractibility
- Disorganization
- Procrastination
- Problems with forethought and judgment

and in some people:

- Lack of impulse control
- Hyperactivity

Having a relationship with someone who is constantly talking or moving about, regularly interrupts you, jumps from subject to subject during a discussion, and seems to have little impulse control can be very frustrating.

ADD is the most common mental health illness in the U.S., affecting five to ten percent of the population. People with this disorder frequently underachieve in school and work, have more family conflict, drug abuse, legal problems, low self-esteem, chronic stress, anxiety, and depression. Luckily, with the help of medication or knowledge and sometimes coaching on coping strategies, clients with ADD can have significantly improved lives and relationships.

Other Impediments to Progress

Holding Back

You may choose to withhold information from your therapist for a number of reasons. While some filtering might be reasonable, or at least understandable, if you've reached a point where you believe you're not making progress, you might ask if there's anything in particular you've been withholding from your therapist. Even if you're uncertain whether it's relevant to moving forward, go ahead and share it, especially if it's something you've been waiting for the "right time" to do.

Resistance to Change

Like most people, you are probably a creature of habit, at least to some degree. Even when faced with a situation or relationship that fails to bring joy, you may cling to it as though without it, you couldn't exist. Sometimes you get stuck with the *idea* of what something could be, or what it used to be rather than what it really is. You resist change even when you know that it's necessary. You are human, after all.

For many of us, change is scary. It's unfamiliar. It's taking a risk without guarantee of reward. Instead of asking yourself what will happen if you continue along, repeating the same mistakes and behavioral patterns that have gotten you into trouble many times before — you ask, "What will happen if I *do* change? Will I lose my family, job, respect in the community, etc.?" There is often fear and anxiety associated with change, even when it's for the better, and there is some level of comfort in the familiar. As the saying goes, better the devil you know than the devil you don't. That's one reason why many people talk about losing excess weight for years but never accomplish their goal. Every time they get close, they panic and go back to their old negative habits.

If you're resisting change, ask yourself what you're getting out of your current situation. You must be gaining something, even if it's painful or negative, or you probably would have done something about it a long time ago. Acknowledging your payoff is the first step in making positive changes.

Additional Reps

In your journal, write down three things you'd like to change about yourself and/or your relationships. Next to each of those three items, jot down the positive changes that might result as well as the negative. For example, if you want to lose weight, a positive change would be improved health and a negative would be cutting out some fattening but tasty foods. Seeing these things in writing may help you determine: What's holding *you* back?

Acting Out

If you've sought therapy for negative behavior patterns and suddenly, after making a good deal of progress in the beginning of your therapeutic relationship, you find yourself relapsing — don't be surprised. Of course, I want you to discuss your behavior with your therapist right away but I also want you to know that this is not necessarily uncommon. If you have used substances — whether it's food, drugs, alcohol, sex or shopping, etc. — as a coping tool for a long time, you may feel out of sorts when you give up that tool. You may even find temporary comfort in returning to your old "friend" (which of course, is not a friend at all). But I'll bet that comfort is very short-lived and unfortunately, you'll probably feel much worse afterwards.

Summing Up

No matter how hard you try to avoid complications, they're part of life. So are mistakes. But there's a bright side to what you may perceive as a "slip" or a step backwards in your therapeutic process: You're learning that this behavior no longer serves you in a positive way. You may even realize that you chose to engage in negative behavior as a way of trying to manage pain or discomfort. In other words, you're making progress. This is just one of several reasons why it's so important to keep working in therapy rather than to assume that it isn't working or that it's done all it can do. And even better news is that you're developing new and positive coping tools to replace old destructive ones. It just takes practice putting them into regular use.

As far as other impediments to your progress such as mood and personality disorders (yours or others'), it's important to seek appropriate support from both professionals and loved ones.

CHAPTER 15

OUR TIME IS UP

Conclusion

In the end, it's not going to matter how many breaths you took, but how many moments took your breath away.
-Shing Xiong

Throughout this book, I've talked about peeling back the layers of the proverbial onion in order to get to the truth. But it's one thing to read about this essential step toward developing and knowing your basic self, or talk about it during therapy — and another to take the time necessary to actually live it. Putting what you've learned in therapy into practice is a daily endeavor. Some days, it will come very easily — almost second nature; other days will be more challenging. But when the proper tools are in place, they are always there for you to use.

How Do You Know When You're "Done" with Therapy?

I've also talked about the difference between simply "feeling better" (which is a good start) and "getting better" (which is healing). When you begin to "get better" you may decide to take a break from therapy. Before doing so, I would suggest discussing it with your therapist. Together, you'll come up with an effective maintenance plan, which may include regular check-ups (many of my clients refer to these as "tune-ups"), or perhaps just an occasional visit when needed for an objective point of view from someone who knows you and with whom you have established a trusting relationship. Sometimes a break from therapy is in order and coming back at a later time may provide a different perspective.

For couples or families in therapy, relationships grow and change over time. There are new challenges that develop and new relationships along with marriages, births and deaths. Therapy can be used as a wonderful tool to deal with all of these situations as they arise. Never be afraid to ask for help or guidance.

Where's MY "Aha Moment"?

Wouldn't it be great if at every therapy session you experienced a sudden insight or realization about yourself that catapulted you to the next level of consciousness? Actually, I say that jokingly because I don't think many of us could effectively process that much information in such a short time. I believe you, quite understandably, would be completely overwhelmed and unsure what to *do* with what you knew.

On television shows, you see therapy clients having breakthroughs every Thursday evening. Perhaps you watch talk shows and celebrity interviews with recaps of "aha" moments that don't always include the length of time (months or even years) or the amount of effort (and number of failures) that it took to reach them. Instead, you witness significant therapeutic progress — something that required concerted effort and full commitment to achieve — in miniscule sound bites: "I was miserable for twenty years; I had an "aha" moment and now I'm ecstatic." If only it were that easy!

In real life, there's a lot more "unfolding" of information and insights than there are revelations. It goes back to the peeling away of the onion's layers; it's gradual and often brings tears along the way. And when the "aha moments" do come, they may not even happen in your therapist's office. Instead, you may have a conversation with your therapist and several days later, an event occurs and you remember something that was said during a session. Something "clicks" for you and you suddenly realize that you're developing a different perspective — a new way of looking at old stuff — and that you have new, helpful coping tools to manage your emotions surrounding the event. Aha!

Summing Up

My sincere hope is that with the aid of this book, alongside your own hard work including self-examination, challenging your core beliefs and growing a basic self, you're beginning to enjoy the fruits of your labor. Regular practice of the topics I discussed including feelings management, journaling, boundary setting, better communication skills and more will allow you to continue in your creation of a very different life from the one you started out with in therapy. You now know that, regardless of your past, you're not stuck with a life that's unfulfilling or overflowing with pain. You have daily opportunities to rewrite your story in a way that gives you peace for the past, joy in the present moment and hope for the future. Talk therapy provides a safe environment in which to purposefully evoke (rather than avoid) memories of your past — even those that are painful — examine them more objectively and then, reshape them. From that point, each time you recall that memory, it no longer automatically brings suffering. It now resides in the compartment of your mind in its new, significantly less painful form.

Talk therapy is also a sacred, extraordinary or even spiritual journey for most people. It allows you to see things in yourself that are profound. The experience between you and your therapist is synergistic in the sense that combined effect of the work you and your therapist is greater than the sum of those efforts if done alone. And the process of therapy is seen as a journey, not as a destination.

What else do you stand to gain in your journey? In a word, *everything*, but if you need specific examples, I am happy to provide them:

- Less anxiety about others' opinions of you — after all, they're just that: opinions.
- A joyous abundance of choices — knowing that you have the power to decide whether or not to continue with things as you have always done them, or try something new and different.

- The ability to take care of yourself without relying on unhealthy behaviors to get you through tough times.
- The knowledge that you're loved, and can love others, just as you and they're.
- And most importantly, more happiness and less suffering.

Learning to look at your life with a fresh pair of eyes and an open heart requires a great commitment. After all, you're not just rewriting your story, you're also learning a new way of thinking and feeling. As you continue your journey in talk therapy, I hope that you will be patient with yourself. My fellow traveler, I wish for you all good things with delight in yourself and in your relationships.

Lift my heart above the pain of former trials.
Remove from me the thoughts that hold me back.
Make clean my heart, make clear my mind, make new my life.

-Marianne Williamson

End Notes

1. "The Johari window, a graphic model of interpersonal awareness", Joseph Luft and Harrington Ingham (Los Angeles: University of California at Los Angeles), 1955.

2. *The Bowen Family Theory and Its Uses,* C. Margaret Hall (Maryland: Jason Aronson, Inc.), 1979

3. Ibid.

4. Ibid.

5. Genogram symbols (*2boundaedia*: Retrieved on June 9, 2015, from http://en.wikipedia.org/wiki/genogram).

6. *Family Therapy in Clinical Practice*, Murray Bowen (Maryland: Rowman & Littlefield Publishers, Inc.), 2004.

7. C. Margaret Hall

8. Ibid.

9. Ibid.

10. *The transtheoretical approach: crossing traditional boundaries of therapy*, James Prochaska, developed with Carlo DiClemente (Illinois: Dow Jones-Irwin), 1984.

11. *Restoration Therapy*, Terry D. Hargrave and Franz Pfitzer (New York: Routledge), 2011.

12. Ibid.

13. Murray Bowen.

14. *Living in the Comfort Zone*, Rokelle Lerner (Florida: Health Communications Inc.), 1995.

15. Murray Bowen.

16. Ibid.

17. Ibid.

18. *Merriam-Webster Collegiate Dictionary*, 11th Edition (Massachusetts: Merriam Webster, Inc.), 2003.

19. *Feeling Good: The New Mood Therapy*, David D. Burns (New York: New American Library), 1976.

20. *Cognitive Therapies and Emotional Disorders*, Aaron T. Beck (New York: New American Library), 1980.

21. *Rational Emotive Behavior Therapy: It Works for Me – It Can Work for You*, Albert Ellis (New York: Prometheus Books), 2004.

22. "Rational Emotive Behavior Therapy", Ann Jorn (*Psych Central:* Retrieved on October 28, 2013, from http://psychcentral.com).

23. *The Ego and the Mechanisms of Defence*, Anna Freud, expanding on the work of Sigmund Freud (London: Hogarth Press and Institute of Psycho-Analysis), 1967. (Revised edition: 1966 (US), 1968 (UK))

24. *Ego Mechanisms of Defense: A Guide for Clinicians and Researchers,* George Eman Vaillant (Washington, DC,: American Psychiatric Press), 1992.

25. "Defense Mechanisms", (*Wikipedia*: Retrieved on October 28, 2013, from http://en.wikipedia.org/wiki/Defence_mechanisms

26. Personal boundaries (Retrieved June 17, 2015 from https://en.wikipedia.org/wiki/Personal_boundaries)

27. Brown, Nina W., Coping With Infuriating, Mean, Critical People - The Destructive Narcissistic Pattern 2006.

28. Rokelle Lerner.

29. Ibid.

30. *Boundaries: Where You End and I Begin*, Anne Katherine (New York: Fireside), 1993.

31. *What Predicts Divorce?*, John Gottman (New Jersey: Lawrence Erlbaum Assoc.), 1994.

32. Brown, B. (2010, December). Brené Brown: The Power of Vulnerability [Video file]. Retrieved from http://www.ted.com/talks/brene_brown_on_vulnerability/transcript?language=en

33. *Diagnostic and statistical manual of mental disorders* (5th ed.), American Psychiatric Association (Washington, DC), 2013.

34. *Embracing the Fear: Learning to Manage Anxiety & Panic Attacks*, Judith Bemis and Amr Barrada (Minnesota: Hazelden), 1994.

For Recommended Reading visit www.insightstherapy.com/index.php/
Recommended-Reading/recommended-reading.html

Made in the USA
Charleston, SC
17 February 2016